An Englishwoman in California

Photograph of Catherine Hubback, probably taken in 1874 by the San Francisco photographer G. D. Morse. (*Gardener deposit, Jane Austen's House Museum*)

An Englishwoman in California

The Letters of Catherine Hubback
1871–76

Edited by Zoë Klippert

Bodleian Library
UNIVERSITY OF OXFORD

First published in 2010 by the Bodleian Library
Broad Street
Oxford OX1 3BG
www.bodleianbookshop.co.uk

ISBN: 978 1 85124 344 0

Designed and typeset in perpetua font (12pt on 14.4pt) by JCS Publishing
Services Ltd, www.jcs-publishing.co.uk
Printed and bound by MPG Books Group, Bodmin and King's Lynn on
80gsm Vancouver Cream Wove
British Library Catalogue in Publishing Data
A CIP record of this publication is available from the British Library

ACKNOWLEDGEMENTS

This book was inspired by the late Diana and David Hopkinson, whose research into the life and work of Catherine Hubback, Mrs Hopkinson's great-grandmother, underlies my own. They welcomed my American perspective, patiently answered my questions, and graciously provided access to unpublished family papers. When I first encountered Catherine Hubback's letters from California, they had been in the collection of the Bodleian Library for more than twenty years. Their significance was recognized by David Vaisey, Bodley's Librarian Emeritus, who was Keeper of Western Manuscripts at the time of their accession. I could not have undertaken this project without his encouragement or sustained it without his support and that of his wife Maureen.

I extend my thanks to members of the Bodleian staff, beginning with Colin Harris, Superintendent of Special Collections Reading Rooms, whose erstwhile stewardship of Room 132, the old Modern Papers Reading Room, made my visits there both productive and congenial. I note also the expertise of Tim Rogers, now retired Deputy Keeper of Western Manuscripts, in analyzing the physical characteristics of the letters. In the preparation of this book, it has been my pleasure to work with Samuel Fanous and others in the Bodleian Library Publishing group: Deborah Susman, Dot Little, Su Wheeler, and former editor Caroline Brooke Johnson, my collaborator across eight time zones.

There are many other individuals whose valuable assistance I wish to acknowledge. Those in England include Tom Carpenter and Louise West, Jane Austen's House Museum; Sarah Lewin and her predecessor Claire Skinner at the Hampshire Record Office; and Diana Gardener, who kindly made possible the publication of Catherine Hubback's photograph. I express my appreciation to Susan McCartan, formerly Honorary Secretary of the Jane Austen Society, for her generosity and guidance.

In California I thank, among others, David Rumsey, Cartography Associates; Kathleen DiGiovanni, Oakland History Room, Oakland Public Library; Alison Moore, North Baker Research Library, California Historical Society; Susan Snyder, Bancroft Library, University of California, Berkeley; Anne Robinson, California Genealogical Society; Robin Doolin, Oakland Museum of California; Susan Grinols, Fine Arts Museums of San Francisco; Jules Kliot and Erin Algeo, Lacis Museum of Lace and Textiles; and Janice Braun, Olin Library, Mills College.

Staff at other American institutions provided valuable assistance: Widener Library, Harvard University; Green Library, Stanford University; San Francisco History Center, San Francisco Public Library; California History Room, California State Library; Oakland Regional Family History Center; Asian Branch, Oakland Public Library; Berkeley Public Library; Alameda Free Library; Sharpsteen Museum of Calistoga History; Hearst Art Gallery, Saint Mary's College of California; and the Moraga Historical Society.

Others, on both sides of the Atlantic, who have contributed to my research are Dr Richard Beidleman, Joe Cody, Susan Leech, David Nicolai, Pam Stutz, Professor Michael Wheeler, and Vicky Wiese.

I am grateful to friends for their encouragement, especially Ulla and Bill Carter, Diana Lindquist, and Edy and Jeff Schwartz. I am grateful as well to my cousins Susan Hendley and Wes Walter, and to my sister-in-law Kay Merseth. My sons Thor and Garth have followed the book with interest and made constructive suggestions.

When people asked if I had a research grant, I said I was supported by a small family foundation. What I did not say is that it consists solely of my husband Jim, who has indulged my early retirement from regular work and willingly accompanied me to the places Catherine mentions in the letters. It is thanks to him that, like her, I moved to California. This book is for him.

CONTENTS

ILLUSTRATIONS

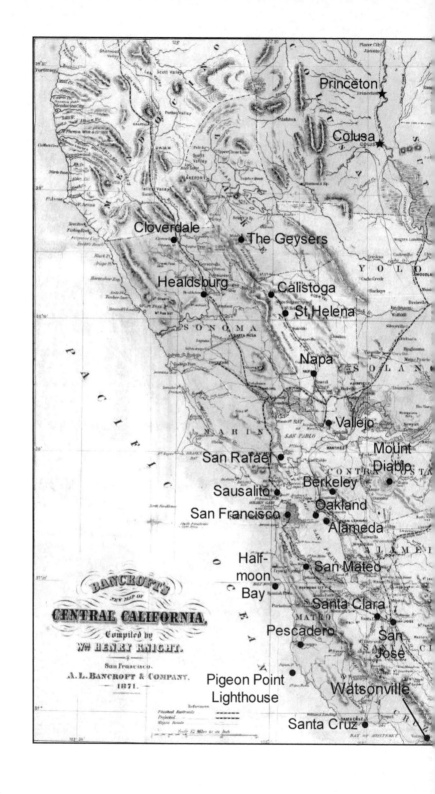

Princeton

Colusa

Cloverdale

The Geysers

Healdsburg

Calistoga

St. Helena

Napa

Vallejo

Mount
Diablo

San Rafael

Berkeley

Sausalito

Oakland

San Francisco

Alameda

Half-
moon
Bay

San Mateo

Santa Clara

Pescadero

San
Jose

BANCROFT'S
NEW MAP OF
CENTRAL CALIFORNIA,
Compiled by
WM HENRY KNIGHT.
San Francisco.
A. L. BANCROFT & COMPANY.
1871.

Pigeon Point
Lighthouse

Watsonville

Santa Cruz

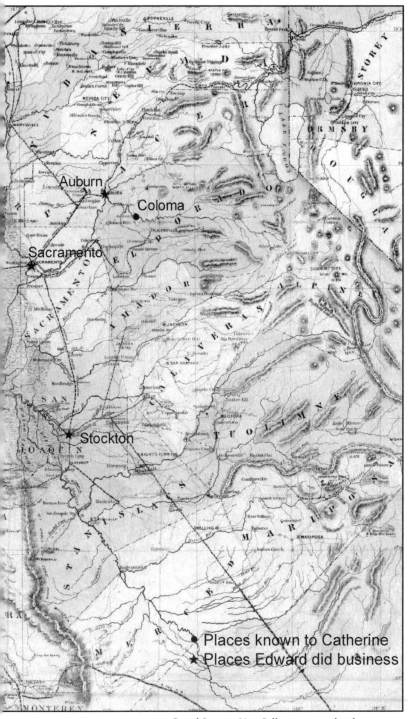

Auburn

Coloma

Sacramento

Stockton

● Places known to Catherine
★ Places Edward did business

David Rumsey Map Collection, www.davidrumsey.com

FOREWORD

In the summer of 1998 Zoë Klippert attended a class which I tutored in Oxford for the University's Department for Continuing Education and the University of California, Berkeley, under the title 'Recovering the Past.' The course, which was based in the Bodleian Library, examined the usefulness and reliability of diaries and letters as historical evidence. During the class, course-members were asked to look at two diaries or small collections of letters—one published and the other unpublished—and to assess their historical importance. From amongst the collections of unpublished correspondence on offer Zoë Klippert chose a group of letters written in California by Catherine Hubback which had been acquired by the Bodleian in 1977.

Having an interest in women's writing and coming herself from the area of California described in the letters, she very quickly saw their significance, both as containing the observations of an articulate woman with literary ability and as contributing to the local history of Oakland in the 1870s.

In the years since 1998 Zoë Klippert has, on both sides of the Atlantic, researched the life of Catherine Hubback—as niece of Jane Austen, as wife and mother, as the author of ten novels in the 1850s and 1860s, and as an immigrant to the rapidly developing town of Oakland on San Francisco Bay in the last third of the nineteenth century. She has now in this book transcribed Mrs Hubback's surviving letters and set them in their context. The result not only slots into place another piece in the Austen family jigsaw puzzle, but is also a significant contribution to the social history of the San Francisco area at a critical time in its development.

The Bodleian Library is delighted to be able to publish the results of Zoë Klippert's dedicated and illuminating research.

David Vaisey
Bodley's Librarian Emeritus

PREFACE

Of Jane Austen's nieces and nephews, Catherine Hubback was the most prolific writer, publishing ten novels between 1850 and 1863. All survive at the Bodleian Library: five in their original two- and three-volume bindings, and five in the one-volume, blue-bound format (covers discarded, margins cropped), whereby minor Victorian fiction was reduced to save shelf space. A thorough analysis of Catherine's novels is beyond the scope of this book, which centers on her life in California in the 1870s.

Unlike her aunt, Catherine Hubback found a ready market, but her success was modest. Only one title went into a second edition, and by the twentieth century most were forgotten or, at best, dismissed for their rambling length and melodrama. By the time I read them—six at the Bodleian and four in pirated editions at Harvard's Widener Library—I was well-acquainted with their author by way of her California letters and inclined to forgive her failings as a novelist. What kept me turning pages (and on occasion cutting them apart) was her rendering of specific places—including those where she lived or visited— and the transportation required to reach them, together with her deft portrayal of characters, many drawn from her own family and friends. It is these attributes that distinguish the letters and enhance their historical interest.

The structure of this book encourages the reader to encounter Catherine Hubback in her letters, as her life unfolded in the 1870s. The introduction provides a context for the letters and a biography from her birth in Hampshire to her arrival in Oakland, California, where the story then continues in her own words. Subsequent events are set forth in an epilogue.

The forty-four letters at the Bodleian represent perhaps a fifth of Catherine's six-year output. Twenty-six were addressed to her son John at his office in Liverpool, and eighteen to his wife Mary at their home across the River Mersey in Rock Ferry. Catherine seems to have assumed that Mary would share her letters with John. By writing to him at his firm, however, she gave him the option of suppressing what might offend his wife. Internal evidence suggests that Catherine wrote to one or the other on an almost weekly basis and expected to hear from them at the same rate. Their side of the correspondence has not come to light, but its regularity and substance are reflected in Catherine's attentive replies.

The surviving letters are unevenly distributed, with recurring gaps of two to six months and a longer break in 1875, when Catherine traveled to England. No pattern of censorship can be discerned. Unlike the surviving letters written by Jane Austen to her sister Cassandra, who famously destroyed many others on grounds of propriety and privacy, Catherine's letters refer freely to family tensions and financial anxieties. They are printed here in their entirety, with minimal commentary. Despite the gaps, their cumulative effect is a coherent view of life in California, in Catherine's distinctive voice, with the occasional jarring lapse into racial or religious stereotyping. While indefensible, such biases can be seen in the context of her circle in Oakland, wherein people of British descent and members of her church predominated.

Information about many of the people and places mentioned in the letters can be found in the sections at the back of the book. The Bibliography, while not exhaustive, provides an overview of the research underlying this edition.

INTRODUCTION

Catherine Hubback was fifty-two years old when she left England for America. The move would increase the distance between her and a family from whom circumstance and temperament had long set her apart. Of the fifteen nieces of Jane Austen to reach maturity, she was the only one to live in an urban environment—six years in London, and eight near Liverpool—and the only one to distinguish herself beyond the domestic sphere. In her thirties, with three young sons, she took up novel-writing and went on to publish ten books between 1850 and 1863.[1]

By the end of 1870 two of her sons were employed in the grain trade. The eldest, John, was a partner in a Liverpool firm, and newly married. His brother Edward, with little hope of advancement in England, had moved to California two years earlier and found employment at a wheat brokerage in San Francisco. Like Edward, the youngest brother, Charles, also sought better prospects in America; he and Catherine sailed from Liverpool on the steamship *City of London*. Their destination was Prince William County, Virginia, where Charles saw opportunities in farming. Catherine continued on to Oakland, California, on the eastern side of San Francisco Bay. Her intention was to foster Edward's career and to make a home for him until he found a suitable wife.

In the years following its incorporation in 1852, Oakland had grown from a scattering of tents and cabins covering a few square miles of marshland to a thriving town of 10,000 people. San Francisco, with a population of 150,000, dominated the region, but Oakland, with lower rents and a culture more suited to families, was an attractive residential community for the middle class. The warmer climate and gentler topography also lured the more affluent, who had profited from the Gold Rush of 1849 and the economic growth that ensued. A regular ferry service, fed by horse-drawn streetcars, made the trip to San Francisco more appealing than it is today.

Larger economic factors were at work as well, driving Oakland's growth. Its proximity to natural resources and arable land made it a commercial hub, where raw materials such as lumber, fruit, and grain were received and processed. It was also the western terminus of the Transcontinental Railroad, completed in 1869. The journey from the Atlantic coast, formerly a matter of months by wagon or weeks by ship and train via the Isthmus of Panamá, was reduced to ten days and could be undertaken in relative comfort. The demographic effect on western migration was predictable and swift. Catherine Hubback, arriving by rail at the beginning of 1871, was part of a new wave of Californians: older, family-oriented, and increasingly female.

Catherine's train delivered her to the Central Pacific depot at 7th Street and Broadway. To the north lay a residential district, where she and Edward would live for the next six years. Like many of their neighbors, including other men of British origin, Edward commuted from Oakland by streetcar and ferryboat. His mother too would rely on public transportation, traveling to San Francisco for shopping and cultural events and to tourist destinations: from Santa Cruz to Sonoma County. She wrote regularly of her experiences in letters to Charles and John.

The letters addressed to Charles have vanished, but forty-four letters to John and his wife Mary were acquired by the Bodleian Library in 1977. Written in a neat hand with few corrections, the letters are full of weather reports and motherly observations. At the same time they are an articulate, detailed commentary on life in California by a novelist and gentlewoman managing a household and finding her place in a new world.

Catherine Hubback would write no more novels, but the letters reflect her flair for characterization and her talent for weaving the stuff of everyday life into a compelling story. As the years go by, they take on a darker tone, as she and Edward suffer the economic reverses of a decade marked by drought, bank failure, and depression. They are nonetheless upbeat and engaging. Neither minor inconveniences nor major Californian concerns such as fires and earthquakes clouded her affection for her adopted home. If her move to Oakland was inspired by motherly solicitude, it was also an opportunity for growth and renewal. The transplantation of two sons to America had dispersed her immediate family. Earlier losses, together with an independent spirit, had already distanced her from siblings and cousins and the quiet gentility of her upbringing.

Catherine Anne Austen was born in Chawton, Hampshire, on 7 July 1818. She was the twenty-sixth of Jane Austen's thirty-odd nieces and nephews, and the first to be born after Jane's death in 1817. Her given names are those of the heroines of her aunt's posthumous books *Northanger Abbey* and *Persuasion*. Her own first novel bears the dedication:

> To the memory of her aunt, the late Jane Austen, this work is affectionately inscribed by the authoress who, though too young to have known her personally, was from childhood taught to esteem her virtues and admire her talents.[2]

2 Mid-nineteenth-century painting of Catherine's birthplace, Chawton House, with St Nicholas Church in the foreground. (*Jane Austen's House Museum*)

Catherine's parents were Jane's brother Francis (called Frank), a captain in the Royal Navy, and his wife Mary Gibson. Catherine was the eighth of their eleven children. At the time of her birth, the family lived at the Great House, Chawton, one of several estates belonging to Frank's brother Edward, who had taken the surname Knight in consequence of his adoption by Thomas Knight, a distant cousin, and his wife Catherine. According to family tradition, Catherine Austen's christening took place beneath a portrait by George Romney of Mrs Knight.

Jane Austen's presence lingered in Chawton, where she had lived her last eight, highly productive, years. The cottage that she shared with her mother, her sister Cassandra, and their friend Martha Lloyd is half a mile from the Great House, and visits back and forth were frequent. The four women had settled in Chawton in 1809, having previously lived in Southampton, where their household included Frank and Mary and their first child, Mary Jane. Jane Austen's letters contain charming glimpses of Frank and Mary and their older children. After Jane's death, her bereaved housemates stayed on at the cottage, in all likelihood lending support at Catherine's birth, and at the birth of her brother Edward eighteen months later.

In 1821 Frank and Mary Austen and their children left Chawton for Ryde, on the Isle of Wight. By July 1823 they had returned to the mainland and were in lodgings at Gosport when Mary gave birth to her last child, a boy named Cholmeley, and died a week later. For Catherine, who had just turned five, the death of her mother was among the earliest of the experiences that would later inform her books. Her sixth novel begins with the death in childbirth of a 'mother . . . in all the prime of womanhood':

> [Her bereaved husband] stepped into the darkened room . . . He opened one shutter a little way; the bright morning sun streamed in upon the white bed-curtains, and danced upon the toilet-glass. He brought his young daughter, clinging to his arms, to the bed, drew back the curtain, lifted the sheet, and [her] eyes fell on the cold, white face . . . [3]

In the novel, the baby dies with his mother:

> on her arm lay the tiny marble face of that little being, whose entrance to this world had cost his parents such a price, and whose stay had been so short, that you wondered why he came at all. [4]

Cholmeley himself would die the following winter, leaving
Frank with five sons and five daughters, aged two to sixteen.
This was a sadly familiar pattern in the Austen family. Three of
Frank's brothers had lost their wives and been left collectively
with seventeen children. When Jane was alive, she was actively
involved in their care and encouragement, as was Cassandra.
For Frank's younger children, the role fell wholly to their
surviving aunt, who paid regular visits.

Compared to his widowed brothers, Frank Austen was well
equipped by temperament, as well as the circumstances of
his career, for fatherhood as a single parent. Having traveled
widely and served with distinction as one of Admiral Nelson's
'band of brothers,' from 1814 he was based on shore. He
appears not to have resorted to the usual remedies of men in
such situations. His brother Edward's measures—governesses
and a large household staff—were beyond his means, and
there is no evidence that he placed any of his children with
relatives, as his brothers James and Charles had done. With
the help of his eldest child, Mary Jane, he held the family
together and continued his active role in their education.

Frank's standards were high, as Mary Jane knew well.
Although her father was at sea for the greater part of her early
childhood, he monitored her progress. 'My dear little girl,' he
wrote from the Baltic to his four-year-old daughter, 'It gives
me great pleasure to hear from your Mamma's letter that you
had improved so much in reading as to be able to read eight
pages . . . at one lesson.' His wife's death left him in full charge
of the schoolroom at Gosport. The atmosphere was lively, as his
sister Cassandra wrote to a cousin in 1827:

> My letter is full of blunders, which require an apology and
> I am sure you will admit the one I am about to make. I am
> at present writing in a room in which half a dozen nephews

and nieces are repeating their different lessons of geography, arithmatic etc and though I must approve of the manner in which they and their father employ their mornings I cannot but acknowledge that a school room is not the most favourable field for letter writing . . .[5]

Catherine, aged nine at the time, was in the middle of a group that ranged in age from six to thirteen; her three eldest brothers had left home. Little more is known of Catherine's education, but approval of her father's methods is implied in her novels, where her treatment of girls' schools is as scathing as her aunt Jane's, and her heroines tend to be educated at home.

An important influence was her aunt Cassandra, who carried on the family practice of reading aloud from Jane's novels—to such effect that, many years later, Catherine's son John would recall his mother and her sister Fanny quoting constantly from the novels and engaging in 'long conversation(s) in terms of the books, never at a loss in finding something suitable.'[6] They were equally familiar with two of Jane's unfinished and untitled manuscripts, of which Cassandra was custodian: the fragments later called 'The Watsons' and 'Sanditon.' Jane had abandoned the first in 1805 and the second in 1817, four months before she died. At some time before Cassandra's death in 1845, Catherine made a copy of 'Sanditon' and perhaps also of 'The Watsons.' The latter would inspire her first novel, *The Younger Sister*. In addition to these works of fiction, Cassandra shared with Catherine and her sisters some of the letters she had received from Jane, which she would later destroy. Their number is unknown, and their content preserved only in excerpts from letters Catherine herself wrote long afterwards.

In the summer of 1828, Mary Jane Austen married a naval officer and moved a few miles north to Fareham. Six weeks

later her father married Martha Lloyd. Cassandra approved of
the union and considered Martha an 'excellent mother to [the]
younger children,'[7] but the reality for Catherine and her siblings
was that their twenty-one-year-old sister had been replaced as
mistress of the Gosport household by a woman old enough to
be their grandmother. At sixty-three, Martha was nine years
Frank's senior, but nonetheless a likely choice as his second wife.
She was an intelligent and resourceful woman, long connected
to the family by virtue of her sister Mary Lloyd's marriage to
Frank's eldest brother James Austen, whose daughters Anna
and Caroline and son James Edward were her own nieces and
nephew, as well as Frank's. During the nineteen years she lived
at Chawton Cottage, she had done her part in nurturing them,
as well as other children of their generation.

Catherine's opinion of her stepmother is not recorded, but
the attitude attributed to her by her descendants is almost
stereotypically that of a high-spirited young woman resentful
of authority and the imposition of eighteenth-century values.
Two characters in Catherine's third novel[8]—a nineteen-year-
old heroine named Kate and her demanding grandmother—
support that view, but the actual relationship may well have
been more congenial. It is hard to imagine that the woman
her late aunt had considered a 'friend and Sister under every
circumstance'[9] could have been wholly unsympathetic.

Beyond the immediate family circle, the marriage of Frank
and Martha had ramifications worthy of a plot by Jane Austen.
A sketch will suffice. The wealthy widow of Frank's uncle
James, Jane Leigh-Perrot found the union 'hard of digestion.'[10]
The result was that Scarlets, the Berkshire estate that the
childless Mrs Leigh-Perrot had promised intermittently to
leave to Frank, passed instead on her death in 1836 to young
James Edward, who adopted the surname Austen-Leigh. For

Frank, the loss of Scarlets was mitigated by a gift from Mrs Leigh-Perrot of £10,000: a sum that enabled him to buy a smaller, better-situated property in the hills above Portsmouth Harbour.

Portsdown Lodge sat in thirty-seven acres, with commanding views toward Spithead and the Isle of Wight. The house required renovation and expansion: tasks which Frank—whose wood-working projects had up till then been confined to toys and furniture—approached with energy, supervising much of the work himself. By early 1831, he had engaged a butler and garden staff and 'made it fit for a gentleman's home.'[11] It was also fitting for a rear-admiral, which he had become in 1830. The atmosphere of the move was tempered by mourning. Frank's third daughter Elizabeth, two years older than Catherine, had died in 1830. He would lose another daughter in 1836, when Mary Jane died at twenty-nine, having borne two daughters and three sons. Their father's failure to provide for his children was of lifelong concern to Frank. When he was well past eighty, he would try to safeguard from creditors the portion of Mary Jane's marriage settlement to which his granddaughters were entitled.[12]

Frank's five sons, in contrast, were a credit to him. Francis and Herbert followed him into the navy, while Henry, George, and Edward went to St John's College, Oxford, on 'founder's kin' scholarships.[13] George and Edward became clergymen, but Henry departed from family tradition and read law. For Catherine and her surviving sisters, Cassandra and Fanny, the comings and goings of the brothers and their friends brought amusement and variety to Portsdown Lodge. Glimpses of their activities are preserved in a sketch book Catherine compiled between 1836 and 1838.[14] The cover bears her monogram, with the 'C' supporting an arrow aimed at a target. Archery was a favorite pursuit, and the Austen family at play was one of the sights of interest to coach passengers on the London to Portsmouth road. A series of sketches entitled 'Young Gentlemen of the Nineteenth Century' are the work of an observant younger sister, with a droll view of temperament and social interplay.

Another set of drawings portray young men at cricket. Three of Catherine's brothers were avid players. A practice pitch was maintained at Portsdown Lodge, and matches were held at the cricket ground in nearby Cosham. In a drawing entitled 'The Marker and the Markee,' a player in a blue-and-white-striped shirt stands before a table furnished with an inkwell and examines a scorecard. Across the table a bonneted woman sits expectantly, pen in hand. In a semi-circle behind the marker, five more women sit framed by a visual pun: the marquee. A likely member of the party was Henry's friend and fellow barrister John Hubback. The two had met in London as early as 1833, when Henry was admitted to the Inner Temple, and both were called to the bar in 1836. A poem Catherine addressed to Henry in July of that year makes gentle fun of his obsession with cricket; a reference to his 'comrade John' suggests that her acquaintance with her future husband had begun.

John Hubback, born in 1811, was the second son of a hat-maker who had served as mayor of Berwick-upon-Tweed. He was the first in his family to enter a profession. Although a university education was the norm among men preparing for the bar, it was not a prerequisite; the three-year residency at one of the Inns of Court, required of graduates, was lengthened to five for non-graduates. For some young men, reading law was an agreeable way to live in London and meet influential people. For others, perhaps Henry Austen himself, it was an alternative to ordination. John Hubback's career path was more straightforward. He seems to have taken full advantage of the opportunity to study case law and to consult with the senior barristers upon whom he would depend for referrals. By the late 1830s he was established in chambers, with a steady supply of briefs.

Class boundaries in private life were more resistant to merit. There were many households, including some connected with the Austen family, where the son of a tradesman would not have been welcome. Frank's opinion of John Hubback is unknown, but he may well have approached his future son-in-law with an open-minded view of upward mobility. The admiral had earned his own way up through the naval ranks, and been awarded the KCB[15] in 1837, with scant benefit of family influence. He was also a pragmatist, with three unmarried daughters. The one most like his sister Jane was Catherine, who was not inclined to hide her intellect in order to attract a husband from the general run of officers and clergymen. The very quality that would intimidate some suitors might be deemed an asset in a barrister's wife.

No record survives of the couple's interaction in the years preceding their marriage, although letters must have been exchanged. John's prose style is preserved in his legal writing, which is clear and engaging. The fullest example of Catherine's writing during this period is a 'Sketch' of Chawton dated 1838.[16] While there is no indication that it was intended for John, it is written as though to a friendly outsider and may well have been part of an ongoing correspondence between two articulate young people from vastly different backgrounds.

The wedding took place on 24 August 1842, with the family gathered at Portsdown Lodge. Catherine's cousin James Edward Austen-Leigh traveled by train from Berkshire to perform the ceremony at Wymering Church. In the evening a violent thunderstorm struck Portsdown, flooding the dining room. Presumably the couple had departed earlier for their wedding trip. Their tour down the Rhine to Wiesbaden was Catherine's only visit to the Continent.

The Hubbacks settled in Bloomsbury. Their house at 42 Torrington Square was a short walk from the British Museum, and less than a mile from John's chambers in New Square, Lincoln's Inn. Their church was Holy Trinity, at the corner of Albany Street and Euston Road. They formed social bonds with John's colleagues and their wives and gave dinner parties that tended, as Catherine would later recall, to 'run away with a great deal of money.' John's income was nonetheless sufficient to support a full household staff, allowing Catherine leisure to explore the cultural resources of London. Two novels set in the city[17] suggest that she made the most of the opportunity, notwithstanding frequent confinements. Her first child, a girl named Mary, lived only long enough to be christened; but three healthy sons arrived in as many years. John's practice flourished, and his *Treatise on the Evidence of Succession to Real and Personal Property and Peerages* was well regarded.[18]

In 1848 the Hubbacks traveled north to see John's family in Berwick and continued on to Scotland. Upon their return John resumed his practice with a court appearance on 29 June. Shortly thereafter he suffered a mental breakdown. Catherine's initial response was optimistic and bold. She closed the London house and moved the family to Malvern, a popular spa town in Worcestershire. They took rooms at Dr Wilson's Hydropathic Establishment, the newly built creation of James Wilson, a physician whose book, *The Water Cure: A Practical Treatise on the Cure of Diseases by Water, Air, Exercise and Diet* may have influenced Catherine's decision.[19] When the doctor's claim to 'have seen insanity cured in a few months' was not borne out in John's case, the family departed for Wales and spent the summer of 1849 in a cottage near Abergavenny.

It was during this difficult period that Catherine began her first novel, completing it in February 1850. By that time she had moved the family to Aberystwyth, apparently hoping the sea air would do John good. Instead, he required constant supervision. His eldest son John, then six years old, remembered his father climbing a cliff from which he had to be rescued. In May a closed carriage brought the family back across Wales to a point on the River Wye where Catherine's brother Henry was fishing. Catherine had arranged for him to intercept the carriage and travel with the family to Gloucester, where they boarded a train that took them into Hampshire. Henry got off with John at Basingstoke and accompanied him to a temporary asylum in Alton. With financial support from fellow barristers, John was subsequently transferred to Brislington House, a Bristol institution run on Quaker principles, where he lived until his death in 1885.

Catherine and the children continued on to Cosham station. Her father's pony carriage met their train and conveyed them up the hill to Portsdown Lodge, which would be their home for the next twelve years. Their arrival increased Frank's ménage to fifteen, including his son Edward, his daughter Fanny, and eight servants. His wife Martha had died in 1843, and his daughter Cassandra in 1849. With Fanny in charge of household affairs, Catherine was free to write her books and to teach her boys, until one by one they went away to school. As the portionless sons of John Hubback, they normally would have been obliged, without undue delay, to earn their living. However, as grandsons of Admiral Sir Francis Austen, each of them received six further years of education, which might, in easier circumstances, have led to professional employment.

Young John went first to Cromwell House, Highgate. Classes were conducted in French, affording him a lifelong facility in the language. The school was otherwise undistinguished, and the family considered sending him to Winchester College, where his uncle George had prepared for Oxford. He went instead to the Royal Naval School at New Cross, which offered a classical curriculum at modest cost to the sons and grandsons of naval officers. His brothers Edward and Charles were enrolled at Cheltenham College, where the registry listed them as sons of 'John Hubback, Esq., Barrister.'

Young John finished school in 1860, the year his grandfather was named admiral of the fleet. Not yet sixteen, he moved to Liverpool, where his father's brother, Joseph Hubback, a successful grain broker, had arranged an apprenticeship for him at the firm of Segar & Tunnicliffe, traders on the Liverpool Corn Exchange. At Christmas Catherine gathered him and his brothers at Malvern, taking the same rooms they had occupied twelve years earlier and leading them on long walks in the surrounding hills. Similarly bracing reunions occurred at Buxton, Matlock, and Rothesay. John lived with his uncle until 1862, when Edward left Cheltenham to assume his own apprenticeship with a cotton broker. Catherine moved north to make a home for them in Birkenhead, across the River Mersey from Liverpool. A prefatory note to her last novel,[20] dated 1 December, was written in lodgings in Hamilton Square. A year later the family moved again, to a house in Church Street, where Charles joined them and went to work in the drafting office of Laird, Son & Company, shipbuilders.

The migration from Hampshire was complete, and the brothers engaged in occupations that were unprecedented in the Austen family. Upon the death of their grandfather in 1865, they made their final trip to Portsdown Lodge, which Sir Francis, retaining a life interest, had sold to the Royal Navy some years earlier. Catherine did not accompany them, and the disposition of the household's contents fell to Fanny. Thus the letters that Jane Austen had written to their parents went with Fanny to Kent and her new home with her brother Edward. Catherine's absence may have stemmed from a desire not to be reminded of the comforts she had left behind. Birkenhead afforded none of the amenities of Portsdown, her home for almost half her life, and little in the way of contact with, in young John's words, 'the professional classes, chiefly naval and legal.'[21] His prosperous employers included her in family parties, but she lacked the means to reciprocate. Her brother-in-law Joseph Hubback contributed to her support, enabling her to be mistress of her own household for the first time in fourteen years, but her modest perch in Birkenhead was uninspiring: 'a patch of houses here and there, with great empty spaces between them.'[22]

A welcome guest in 1864 was William Ingram, whose acquaintance with the family dated from his tenure as curate at Wymering, and whose sister Mary was a favorite with Catherine. Mr Ingram was on his way to Kirk Michael on the Isle of Man, and a new appointment as vicar. He would be joined by Mary and his mother, who in 1865 made their own visit to Church Street, with the predictable result that John, then twenty-one, fell in love. His five-year apprenticeship was at an end and his prospects good, but two years elapsed before he spoke of marriage. The catalyst was his firm's decision to send him to Australia in pursuit of wheat to offset poor harvests elsewhere. With an absence as long as three years before him, he proposed and was accepted. Catherine's approval is evident in a letter to Mary, dated 23 October 1867: 'how glad I shall be to receive you as a daughter.'[23]

When John arrived at Adelaide in mid-December, he learned that he had made the trip for nothing. His assessment might have been written today: 'The hot winds from Central Australia had ruined the ripening wheat crop, and there was no exportable surplus.'[24] A telegraph connection had not yet reached Australia, and he waited several months for instructions to proceed to California. His month-long voyage ended at the Gulf of Panamá, where he boarded a coastal steamer for San Francisco. He reached the city at the end of June 1868 and found lodging across the bay in Oakland. Knox House on Telegraph Avenue offered room and board in a country setting a mile to the north of the commercial district. Meals were supplied in part from the adjoining garden and orchard, and breakfast was served early to accommodate commuters. John's assignment was to monitor the wheat crop in the Central Valley and report by telegraph to his employers, who furnished him with letters of introduction to their counterparts in San Francisco. His trips to the city were geared to business hours in New York and Liverpool, and his afternoons were devoted to sightseeing. He saw good prospects in the grain trade for his brother Edward and secured a clerkship for him at Dickson, DeWolf, & Company, commission merchants, on Battery Street.

Edward traveled to California by way of Panamá and joined John at Knox House in mid-September. On 21 October his morning walk to the streetcar was interrupted by a tremor on the Hayward Fault: the strongest earthquake theretofore recorded in California, and the subject of a letter to his mother two days later.[25] 'When it was over,' he wrote, 'I felt so weak with fright that I could scarcely walk'—but walk he did, and finding the streetcar service suspended, he continued on foot to the wharf, boarded the nine o'clock boat, and reached San Francisco at ten, little more than an hour later than his usual arrival time. John learned of the earthquake in Victoria, British Columbia, where he had gone on business. He returned in time for a strong aftershock on 5 November. No one at Knox House was injured, but a chimney fire broke out early the next morning. The building burned to the ground, and most of John's possessions were destroyed. He had already made plans to return to England and left Oakland two weeks later, taking a Wells Fargo mail coach to Wyoming Territory, a succession of trains to New York, and finally a steamer to Liverpool.

In John's absence, Catherine and Charles had moved to Rock Ferry, a suburb to the south of Birkenhead. From their modest house at 3 Victoria Road, they looked across a field and railway cutting to a neighborhood of larger dwellings. The longer ferry ride to Liverpool, with 'opportunity for the exchange of greetings and politics,'[26] was agreeable to John, who resumed his duties at Segar & Tunnicliffe and attained a partnership in August 1869.

John's return to England coincided with the preparation of a book about Jane Austen by Catherine's cousin James Edward Austen-Leigh. *A Memoir of Jane Austen* quoted letters that Jane had written to him and to several nieces, including his sister Caroline Austen and his half-sister Anna Lefroy. James Edward's approach to Catherine's sister Fanny met resistance—she would let him read the letters to her father, on condition that they not be published; but 'when pressed by Mr Austen-Leigh,' she destroyed those to her mother, which Frank had kept for more than forty years. 'She was not within her rights,' her nephew John observed, 'the letters were the property of my mother as the elder sister.'[27] The *Memoir* was published in December 1869 and favorably received. A second edition was in progress when

James Edward received two letters from Catherine, dated 1 and 14 March 1870. Her apparent purpose, as reflected in a surviving excerpt, was to augment his account of Jane's refusal of a proposal from a 'gentleman' by drawing on her own recollection of the letters that Cassandra had allowed her to read:

> I gathered from the letters that it was in a momentary fit of self-delusion that Aunt Jane accepted Mr Wither's proposal, and that when it was all settled eventually, and the negative decisively given she was much relieved.[28]

James Edward's reply, if any, is unknown; but the second edition of the *Memoir* contains no acknowledgment of Catherine and no evidence of her contribution. By the time of its publication in 1871, she would be far away in California.

The intervening year was one of realignment for the Hubbacks. With the sudden death of a senior partner in March 1870, John's financial interest in the firm became sufficient to support a household. He and Mary Ingram set 4 October as their wedding date. In the interim, Catherine planned her departure. John would later describe his mother's decision in terms of family dynamics:

> I had for a long time recognised that my brother Edward was more in sympathy with my mother's modes of thought and action than I had ever been myself . . .
>   To be sure, I had my own Mary to think of, at all times, and I may have been less ready to accept my mother's points of view. Gradually it came to be understood that when I was married and settled, she would go to be with Edward . . .[29]

Also understood was that John and Mary would settle in the Rock Ferry house where Catherine had lived for two years. The ceremony took place at William Ingram's church at Kirk

Michael, with Mary's younger brother Arthur officiating. The couple returned from their wedding trip in time to see Catherine and Charles off to America. For three weeks all four lived together. 'It was not,' John recalled, 'a happy time for myself nor indeed for Mary.'[30] A story persisted in later generations that Mary resented her mother-in-law's continuing to sit at the head of the table and pour the tea.

If Catherine in turn felt resentment at being displaced, her letters do not betray it. If her move, like those preceding it, was driven by necessity, it was in equal measure an opportunity to redefine herself. The Oakland *City Directory* of 1872 lists her as a widow. The persistence of the designation in subsequent editions suggests it was Catherine's choice and not an error. Her husband's illness had determined the course of her life for more than twenty years. She had adapted to diminished status and succeeded as a single parent, but the collapse of her marriage was difficult to talk about, especially with new acquaintances. By styling herself a widow, she might sidestep painful conversations.

The Letters

Letters from Catherine Anne Hubback, née Austen, in Oakland, California, to her son John and his wife Mary in Liverpool, 1871–6. (MS. Eng. lett. e. 150)

July 1871–July 1872

In anticipation of his mother's arrival, Edward Hubback had moved from a furnished room to a rented house at the northwest corner of 11th and Grove Streets. The wood-framed Italianate bungalow was smaller than its neighbors, but dignified and well-proportioned. The markets on Washington Street were a short walk away, as was St John's Episcopal Church, where Catherine would find a social network and a source of amusement at American ways.

~ 1 ~

July 9th [1871]
Oakland

My dearest John,

I did receive yours and Mary's letters on the evening of the 6th, and so you made a pretty correct calculation. Many thanks to you for your good wishes, and I return them to you both with all my heart. Perhaps some day I may be in England again on the 7th of July, but you know I have been about in various places at that time very often.

3 Early twentieth-century view of the house at 11th and Grove Streets, Oakland, where Catherine lived from 1871 to 1873. The trees at the far left of the photograph obscure the block's only nineteenth-century survivor, the Pardee residence (1868), now the Pardee Home Museum. (*Courtesy of the Bancroft Library. University of California, Berkeley*)

Everybody here encourages me to suppose that I have no chance of leaving this place for 15 years at least—so I shall be pretty old in that case—before I see you again. If I do reach England again I am sure I shall never like living there, unless I can get into some very warm sunny corner somewhere. If Edward left San Francisco it would be a reason for my leaving of course, but I like this place and climate much too well to leave, and nothing but necessity would make me *settle* in the neighbourhood of Liverpool—I agree with Edward in feeling I never knew how much I hated it until I got away.

I am glad your garden flourishes. It is no merit to me watering with a pot, because if we had a hose we might not use it, unless we had a well too, and when Mr Emerson will really see about that I do not at all know. We have ice, so we can make the water drinkable, but it is quite warm in the middle of the day from the sun.

We had a very pleasant holiday on the 4th. Edward would not go to a picnic, but stayed at home to take me out. Days before the air had reverberated with preparatory crackers and bombs, and the preceding night I think they were letting them off until daylight, to say nothing of a drum which a boy neighbour of ours practised incessantly as long as I was awake—so I had but little sleep that night.

I was rather glad we had not to get up very early. We had intended to go to San Rafael, which would have obliged us to be out at 7:45—but the boats did not run, so we resolved to go and see San Jose where Edward had never been. Accordingly we took the train there at 9:30—and reached it about 12—the train taking it very easy all along. We went into the town on foot, notwithstanding the coaches so temptingly decked with U. S. flags of all sizes! It had been cool when we left Oakland, but oh how hot it was at San Jose—the ground burnt one's feet, and gave out heat as strongly as the sunbeams. But I like heat, and can take a great deal without harm.

We found almost everybody who was not at the park or gardens sitting in best clothes in the street to look on. I suppose there was to be something to be seen, but I don't know—we did not see anything extraordinary. We had some soup, and tart and fruits by way of lunch at the best hotel, and were extremely amused at the friendly and familiar tone of the discourse between 3 boarders, and the waiter. The two ladies liked the heat and enjoyed San Jose, the two gentlemen, especially the waiter detested it and wished themselves back in the City The thermometer stood over 100° in the shade in the middle of the day.

Then we went out at a venture, and got into a car which took us to Liveoak Park, a not very tempting place, all full of swings and crackers, beer and bands of music—so we walked back to make another start. Next time we did get the right vehicle, for we wanted to go along the Alameda to Santa Clara. There's a tramway, and street cars run, and we inserted ourselves in one and started—we picked up numbers of people every two or three minutes, all well dressed, smiling, cheerful and obliging. Presently we were quite full, so when some more got in some of the men stood up to give the women seats, then as more came by degrees *all* the men stood, then more, and the children had to sit on laps—then more, and they *had* to stand too, then more, and they had to wait outside at one end or other, because it was impossible to squeeze closer. Everybody was as cheerful as possible, chattering and laughing—and along the beautiful long avenue we went until at last we came to some gardens where was a pond and two little boats, holding 3 or 4 people paddling about where they had about room to turn round.

This was the bourne of most of the travellers, and the lines of buggies, waggons and vehicles of all descriptions drawn up under the trees in double and treble rows for about a ¼ of a mile, showed that there was something very attractive there. However we stuck to the car, determined to see as much as we could for our money, and went right on to Santa Clara, where the car waited 20 minutes and then returned. We walked about and looked at the outside of the college, and then came away, as our train was to leave as we thought at 3:30. We had just the same sort of thing coming home, only the car got off the track, and had to be unloaded to get it on, and the crowd which scrambled down, and poured out was really wonderful. We were too early after all at the Station and as they were painting the waiting room we had no place to sit down on, and I could not get a cup of tea. I was very thirsty, as we had only a tumbler of ice at the hotel, and I can't drink ice, *pur et simple*, tho' I like the water cooled.

However we reached home about 6:30, and as we had given Cah a holiday, we proceeded to get tea ourselves, I lighting the fire, and boiling water and Edward laying the table. We not infrequently do this, and always know where to find things, which is a great comfort.

Then Edward went down to Kelsey's to see the fireworks. I was not asked so I stayed away. I thought the Woolseys or Mrs Kelsey herself might have asked me—unless they thought my English feelings would be hurt by the demonstration—but Edward went. Mr Knox had fireworks and supper too—there were fireworks all round everywhere—one could not help seeing some look where one would. The Kelsey people had a grand demonstration—they made a procession, the ladies all masked with towels or something, the gentlemen carrying brooms with dusters, and napkins as flags, or shovels, or fire irons—the senior lady ringing the large dinner bell, somebody beating the gong, and the others making what noises they best could. 150 people walked 2 × 2 in this order from Kelsey's and Knox's all down Telegraph road, and paid their respects to the other boarding house. I suppose they *are* all sane, but they must have looked like a company of lunatics. The supper table they say was very pretty, all flowers and tricolored ribbons. Last Sunday [breaks off, no second sheet]

~ 2 ~

My dearest John,

I am longing for another letter from you to tell me how your wife and daughter are going on. I had one written on Sunday after the event and have not had any news since, so that it is now almost 4 weeks—no, quite 4 weeks—since the great event, and I hope Mary is quite well by this time. I suppose I must wait till she can write to me before I get any description of the baby, and by that time its eyes and nose will have begun to develope. Does Mrs Ingram think like the lady I heard once say when her son was asking—'Now mother, is it not the finest child you ever saw?'—who answered, 'My dear I was a mother before I was a grandmother!' I do want to know all about it however, and what name you intend to give it, and all the rest.

I have been much taken up last month visiting Mrs Hudson who has a severe illness. She is better now, and able to get out again. She is a very near neighbour, at the next corner of 11th Street, and English, and very nice and I am very fond of her.

I went last week to the Fair[1] at San Francisco, which you know is a small 'Great Exhibition.'[2] Of course to Californians, or Statistical minds it is interesting as it is really all the various stores assembled in one place but then I don't care for looking at furniture or cloth or pickles and preserves or even machinery or carriages. The Japanese and Chinese stores interested me most. There are the loveliest things there. They may be sold, but cannot be had till the fair closes, as one does not pay for them. I found a small teapot, a little smaller than my Pompeian one, and 6 cups of finest porcelain irresistible. The cups are all this shape and size [sketch] and are white with a red lobster on them. They are perfectly charming and only cost $1.50, which is so cheap! The very finest ware was only $1.75, and that as it happened was sold—but I liked my shapes the best. The Japanese interpreter was not there, so I could not tell the prices of his things, but I want some of the silks, and other things and mean to go again, and find out if they are as cheap in proportion. Japan silk here is $1.50 a yard which is much higher than in England—but being cheap compared to French silk, it is not valued at all. You know how I like porcelain and Japan ware.

I have been disappointed at not getting a box sent to you, but at Oakland Wells Fargo[3] put every possible obstacle in the way of sending anything, and it ended after they had it a week, in Edward's taking it under his arm and carrying it off again. They charged so enormously—so it will go by a ship next week, whose Captain will take it for Edward. There is a little Japan Cabinet for Mary which I hope she will like—and a pearl shell[4] for a photo frame cut and polished for you—but I cannot get a gilt moulding for the edge, so I am sorry I cannot sent it perfectly—but Mr Mayer will fit it for you easily, and there is a *siempre vivens*[5]—or some such thing in a little case, which you know you must put in a source of water, and it will all come out green and beautiful ever so soon. There are some fossils which Charlie wants to have sent to the Cheltenham museum when you have a chance, which I want to put in, as the box is going by sea, and weight will not signify, and two little Japanese tea-boxes, for the Reading little girls, which I must trust you to pack up and send on. I wish I could send it quicker, but at any rate I hope you will get it by Xmas at least—if not by your birthday, which I suppose is not likely. Those little Japan cabinets delight me so, I should like to have half a dozen of them.

We have a touch of warm weather at last, and today it really is quite hot and thirsty. Mr Oxland lunched here after Church today—he is living in the City now, and so is Mr Holderness who wanted to come and board here, but we have no room furnished, and don't mean to have. I use the spare room as a workshop and cannot spare it—tho' I should like sometimes to have a spare bed for a friend like Mrs Norris[6]—you know.

Have you read 'Lady Susan'[7] which is the name of E. A. Leigh's second edition? I wish he would send me a copy! but I have been so unlucky as to see the last 2 moons through the window pane, so have had no chance of wishing. Your Aunt Fanny[8] is at Maplestead, and I suppose your Aunt Frank[9] to be at Reedvale, Teignmouth. She has been at Leamington, and saw Stoneleigh—going over the inside. She was much struck by the grandeur of the house inside, and the oaks, and wonders our great-uncle sold it.[10] If he had not, and if things had been different, it might have come to your grandfather you know. She says the old portrait of Old Sir T. Leigh strongly reminded her of some of the living members of the family—Herself perhaps—as she has a Leigh face.

I am sorry to hear no better account of your Uncle H[11] at Reading and his family. The only fault California has is that it is so far off—if I could only have a visit now and then from Georgie Harden, or Kate Lee, or see Sister Pauline about whom your Aunt Fanny raves, or your Aunt herself—it would be perfect. How she would enjoy the bananas, peaches, grapes and pears in which we revel. One gets 3½ lbs of best grapes or peaches for 2 bits. I have been eating a banana whilst writing this.

They are going to have a sacred concert in the Church[12] on Thursday evening in aid of the funds. They had one (a profane one I suppose) last week in aid of the other Church in Brayton Hall, and we went, but I don't like going to one in a Church.

They are going to have a fair also, for the other, which is the other side of Broadway. Mrs Martin is going to ask me to work for it, but I shall not. I don't like bazaars.

Pray give my love to your wife and daughter and regards to Mrs Ingram and believe me

Your affectionate Mother
Catherine A. Hubback

3

September 24th [1871]

My dearest John,

I hope you had a pleasant tour, and fine weather. I shall like to hear where you went, and all about it. It would do Mary good to get a little of the Ozone of Michael.[13]

I hope you are not tormented with gnats, we are, and they are monsters—not real mosquitoes but large gnats [sketch] as big as that. They have stung me on the ankles. I think they come in the evening, or perhaps when I go out in shoes in the garden, and they are so swollen (my ankles), I can hardly walk, and could not bear any boots today, but have been lying on the sofa dabbing arucia[14] on my feet nearly all day.

Mr Holderness came in whilst Edward was at Church, to go with him to Alameda, to the afternoon service there,[15] where he sings—they sang Nazareth:[16] it would be more appropriate 3 months hence, but it is new out here—nobody knew it, until I spoke of it to Mr Holderness, and then they got it at Alameda.

I have a very enthusiastic admirer just now, a recent acquaintance who has fallen in love with me—but you need not be afraid of scandal as it is only a tall young lady, Miss Leila Kirkham, one of the leading belles of Oakland. She is a little odd and wild, but very clever, and has been in England—and likes English things and people. Her father General Kirkham whom I don't know, has rather spoilt her—and her mother like other American mothers is of course nothing and nobody—so Leila has pretty much her own way, but she is not in the Taunton style at all—and the Taunton girls whom she met at Mrs Littledale's at Liskeard scandalised her a good

4 *Oaks at Madison and 8th Streets* is the work of Ferdinand Richardt, who
settled in Oakland in 1876, the year of Catherine's departure. He painted
scenes well known to her, including this intersection near the home of
the Kirkham family. (*Ferdinand Richardt, Danish American, 1819–1895,
Oaks at Madison and 8th Streets, c.1877, Collection of the Oakland Museum
of California, Gift of Mr Lester M. Hale*)

deal. She met Mr Goodwin in India too. She has been learning
some lace stitch of me to make spiders—but she calls them
bugs—as Americans call all insects.

My story[17] has come out in the October *Overland*,[18] but I
have not received any money yet. I am anxious to know how
much they will pay—I have two more ready, but I don't write
for nothing—by and bye they can be all put in a volume and
published again. I mean in future to have my name printed Mrs
C. Austen Hubback and make believe the A. stands for that. I
never have written it *at length*—so nobody knows, and Austen
is a good *nom de plume*.

Have you seen or heard of E. A. Leigh's volume—Lady
Susan—I think he is mean not to send it to me—very mean
and real ugly, and I feel quite bad about it and shall not have a
good time till I get it. I am real mad (not that I am a bit—but
those are Californian expressions). He has not said the first
thing about sending it. I have to keep my *Californianica* aired,
for use in my stories, so I practise it on you.

Edward and Mr Holderness dined at Alameda so I dined
alone, and ate a lamb chop, tomatoes, sweet potatoes and a cob
of corn, which I think the best part of dinner—and I kept the
apple tart for tomorrow uncut. I can make very good pastry
now—and often surprise Edward with some entirely new and
original pudding. When I do make a pudding in the kitchen
Cah always comes and sweeps the drawing room, so I might
say—'The lady's in the kitchen baking the ripe plums, the man
is in the parlour sweeping up the crumbs.' What nonsense I am
writing—I wonder at it.

If you went away on the 11th that was just when the
Wedderspoons reached Liverpool, and now *she* is dead—how
sad for him and her children. Mrs Hudson thinks they will
come back again now—but it is so sad to die in a strange
place at an inn, like the Adelphi. Still he must be glad he tried
everything—if she had died here, which she certainly would
have done, he might have thought going to England would have
saved her.

Has Charlie told you about his love affairs—'if not, don't
say I did'—but he is, as far as I can make out, as good as
engaged to Mrs Heenicker's sister—whose name happily is
'Bernhardine'—quite a new name in the family which I am
thankful for.[19] Of course he must wait till the mill runs all right,
but he is as old as you were, Sir, when you fell in love—and
as likely to do well. I am glad it is not an American girl—tho'

I don't expect Charlie will return to live in England—still there's a chance, and I don't think any American girl would be happy there.

We are looking forward to the promised rain of September to wash away a little dust and cobwebs, but I suppose we must not hope for much—and people are beginning to talk of earthquaky sensations and fears for next month. There have been 2 tremendous fires—half Virginia City is burnt down, which is a loss from insurance of $100,000—and a block in San Francisco last night, on Market street, of great value, 3-story houses quite destroyed—wholesale warehouses. Just now when everything is so dry, it makes one nervous about fire and candles, and so forth—when one lives in a bandbox and has a Chinese servant besides—not but what Irish women are just as careless.

I have sent 2 painted photos for sale to the City. Mr Watkins thought I should most likely sell them, I only want $15 apiece— that is fine for my own work. I saw the moon last Sunday as we were going to Church and turned my money so I hope to get it. The nights are lovely, and the mornings delicious until the sun gets too hot—and plants are growing again, and blowing again as if they expected rain.

I hope Mary will send me particulars about the little daughter—how she grows, and crows, laughs and cries.

So now I shall finish. My feet are tired of being down—so with love to you both

Goodbye

Your affectionate Mother
Catherine A. Hubback

4

December 25th [1871]
Oakland

My dear Mary

I am glad the socks please you. You shall have more of them in time for your daughter to wear, and I will take care and make them larger as you say.

We have had such a wet and stormy week as you can form no idea of in England. It began to rain on Sunday night, and stopped on Wednesday about noon for a short time. With a few heavy storms at intervals it held up until Friday evening when it began again, and rained all night and nearly all Saturday. Not small rain, but cascades and cataracts. There have been floods in nearly every home in Oakland, our leak being chiefly over the dining room chimney. I have had to put pans and dishes and cloths instead of a hearth-rug, and when I went to make up the fire had great drops falling on my head. I suppose it is not over yet, but we should be glad not to have the rain all at once, needful as it is. Last year the rainfall was 10 inches short of the average, but it has already exceeded last year's fall by several inches—and as we have just begun, we expect to have enough to make the balance even. It is so important for the country that one must bear it with satisfaction—and we have got through *one* week of the 3 we may expect. Is it not odd it should come punctually every 10 years in this way? Everything is as green and fresh as in April in England, the acacias are all coming out, and the coral trees and the great white arums, and Australian plants generally, in fact. One can't realise that it is Xmas.

We got through our Church Festival very well—the fear of rain kept some people away, the first night, but there was a beautiful moon and no rain. So the next night a great many more came, and it poured as we went home. The way in which it all sinks in and disappears half an hour after it stops raining, altho' everything had been under water before, quite surprises me. There's a huge lake in Grove Street, just in front of our gate, which is about up to the horses' knees, and extends the whole length of the block, but it swells when it rains to such an extent that I expect in a little time we shall be quite on an island—it does not matter much because I don't go out when it is raining often, but Edward had to wade on Saturday the whole way to the Station. The railroads all about the country have been washed away, and communication stopped. At San Rafael they have been quite cut off, and Mr Makin having gone up in a buggy, which refused to take him through the water, had to wade to his gate, up to his knees, and fell into a hole in the road, narrowly escaping drowning. So the buggy was right to decline driving there.

We had a very good time at the Festival, there were dinners and suppers, oysters, punch, lemonade, flowers, dancing, music, tableaux and so forth. I really liked it. I had never seen *tableaux* before, and some of these were very well got up. One of Guido's *Aurora*,[20] with the 12 dancing horses was really beautiful. The horses of course were invisible but she was holding the reins, and 12 children were the horses—seen by a red light, and then a yellow, and finally a white one—it was as pretty as you could fancy.

Edward acted in one, as a pirate, but he afterwards discarded his dress, which consisted only of a hat and my crimson cloak, the other pirates retained theirs for the evening—Mr Oxland appearing in a coloured shirt, and high boots over his trousers, a belt with dagger and pistols, and a scarlet Neapolitan or Greek cap—which had a remarkable effect on his long thin figure when he was dancing. The Miss Bacons were the chief actresses—one was Juliet awaking in the tomb—one was Perdita, at the unveiling of the statue. Ella was the young wife with an old husband nodding on one side of her, and her lover on the other kissing her hand—which was encored and applauded until she could not stand it any longer, but snatched away her hand from her cousin, bowed to the audience, and the curtain fell amidst peals of laughter.

The American girls carry themselves so badly, owing to the exaggerated Grecian bend, that they all look humpbacked, and *poke* frightfully as we used to be told when we stooped our heads and rounded our shoulders—it is very different from the fashionable carriage when the same style of dress prevailed formerly—when 'to bridle properly' was an art taught in the nursery. I remember Mrs Port of Ilam writing to her Aunt or Mother, Mrs Delany, and saying her little girl 'began to bridle very prettily.' When they curtsey the girls here look like ducks waddling into the water, you know how they go off—and when they dance they are about as graceful as so many cows—not that they could not dance if they chose (tho' they can't walk a bit) but because they think stooping forwards, setting up their shoulders and going head foremost is 'the thing.' They copy anything French, and I am told that as those who went to Paris had more opportunity of studying what is now called the *demie-monde*, than anything in good society, the dress as well as the manners of living and thinking are adopted from them. Perhaps if their costume were Grecian, the bend might not be so unbecoming, but with all the bunch of panniers and bustle, and overskirt, and enormous sash bows they are more like Christian[21] with his burden on than anything else. Are English

"Nature ... studies from"

5 Three views of a fashionable young woman entitled 'Studies from Nature,' featuring 'the exaggerated Grecian bend.' (*MS. Eng. lett. e. 150, fol. 10r*)

girls all fallen into the same way of walking, hobbling and poking? I send you some sketches on the other side illustrative of the style here. I hope you will have been to the Fancy ball. It seems always a pity to decline an invitation, unless going is quite out of the question, because it cannot matter a straw at a ball whether one person is absent who was expected, so you can always stay away if necessary.

The stormy weather interfered very much with dressing our Church, as flowers were mostly drowned, and trees too wet to cut or bring indoors. Edward and Mr Oxland and Mr Henderson did the best they could on Saturday evening—but none of the young ladies who were expected came. However this morning (Xmas) they came and brought some flowers, and the altar was dressed with great white arums and green boughs, and laurustinus which is a sort of exotic here and much valued.

I hope you and John and your 'young one' will have a happy Xmas and New Year and all my old friends at Rock Ferry— only I believe they are nearly all gone. However there is Mrs Bradbourne to whom I send good wishes, and I don't remember anyone else, who is not gone away.

I wonder how Charlie feels today—as John did on the 1st of October 1870.

Believe me

> Your affectionate Mother-in-law
> Catherine A. Hubback

[postscript] Pray send my best Xmas wishes to all at Michael when you write.

5

January 7th
1872

My dearest John,

Many thanks to you both for Lady Susan, who arrived last night safely. I had great fears for her on her journey on account of the present state of flood and snow on the route. It delayed everything, but at last a way has been forced through, and your letters came on Friday and the book on Saturday. I like the photograph of the Baby particularly, and Mary in it, better than the single one of her. Baby is just like what Edward was at that age. Thank you both—your letters were dated December 7 so they were a whole month coming—and Charlie's last letter is dated 15—so I know nothing about what he has done since.

Still now the road is open again, I hope to have a letter from them this week, saying they are really married. Until then I shall be constantly afraid something has interfered. Bernhardine wrote to me at last, a charming little natural affectionate letter. I hope it will all be a good thing for them both. Think of its all coming from our sailing in that *City of London*. I wonder what Charlie would have done otherwise.

I hope you have had my last week's letter about the money. The last premium must have been paid now, and I know that was £28. The £45 which I had p. an. from my Mother[22] used to pay them both. That will be now free—but I want to know exactly what I have a year—surely more than £28 a quarter, as you say. It used to be £60 half-yearly, and there ought now to be £22 more or thereabouts which would be £40 a quarter I suppose allowing for income tax—or thereabouts. If we cannot have the principal, I do wish to have the interest regularly and punctually, which can only be done by getting Mr Heath to give up personally reviewing the DWs[23]—but having them paid to your banker or agent or in some business- and purpose-like way. I don't see why we must wait his pleasure and convenience, when we could do without him, and waiting loses us money.

But I am very correct indeed in wishing to have some of my money (all if I can) out here. If Edward could get £2,000 this spring he could go into business this year, which will be a good one, and he would never have so good an opening—but without a capital he can do but little or nothing indeed—and it seems so hard that my money cannot be made of any advantage to him. There's no risk in investing money here, at reasonable interest, as you know—and of course I should be glad to have a little time of easy competence, after so many years of economy and struggle—but I would not care about that even, if I could see Edward in a way of independence. £2,000 would be less than his future share if my money is equally divided amongst you, as I always intend it should be, if I have anything to do with it—and if he could have that he could of course engage to reckon it as part of his share, and in case I do not survive to make a will (which you know I cannot do unless I am a widow) he could undertake not to claim more than what would make a third, so you would neither of you be the worse.

If he took a share in a business, it would be a commission business, which he could get with this money this year, so there would be no risk, and you know how he hates speculation—he has other little plans too in his head which would help without risk—but I have a strong idea that when it comes to the point Mr Heatley will not part with him, and if he will make it worth Edward's while to stay he will not object—in which case his capital might remain until he wanted it—but without something as a *point d'appuie*, he cannot make any more. He is of so much importance in the office, and has so much of Mr Heatley's confidence that I can't see how they can do without him—but I can't go to Mr H. as I did erstwhile to Mr Segar, and say he must understand that unless a sufficient salary were given he must seek one elsewhere. Mr Carlin got a situation, with a small salary but a prospect on [sic] increase. Mrs C. is a hardworking body, who is used to do all her own household work, and as such living here is not really hard, because the climate and manners are alike easy and accommodating.

I have crowded my garden with plants, slips, cuttings and roots of all kinds. I have such numbers of geraniums, fuchsias, and abutilons, verbenas of all colours, growing in wild luxuriance—a young hedge of chrysanthemums of various colours—and many plants quite unknown in England. I don't know how many I shall have to root out by and bye—but I do like filling it. It is splendid weather for gardening. We have one sunny day, then two or three cloudy ones, and since I sowed a pint of peas yesterday, two long rows—peas here don't care for sticks, despising such vanities—I suppose they will come up next week—my hyacinths are all out of doors.

I only wish I could show you both my room. It really is so pretty and full of fancies. Mr Emerson, our landlord's brother, and next neighbour rather likes to come in here and pay me a visit, he says he knows nobody who has so much invention—and he wanders about the room admiring all my contrivances—his little girl on New Year's day seeing her mother about to drink a glass of wine, burst out crying—'Oh Mama don't take that, you will get drunk'—and howled vigorously. That is turning the tables is it not—Miss Bell being about 7 years old.

Edward and I have just undertaken to teach in the Sunday school. It is not bad—I had a rather nice class of 8—there will be more however on a fine Sunday——it was too threatening today. There are about 100 nominally in the school, and were only 4 teachers who come regularly. I hope we shall be able to do so——as it is only 5 minutes walk, and no school on wet Sundays.

I would like to see you as Duke of Buckingham.——I have no doubt Mary is right as to your appearance. I conclude she is not going. I am glad she has a nice nurse. I shall soon send some more socks.

Goodbye and love to you both and the little one.

Your affectionate Mother
Catherine A. Hubback

~ 5.5 ~
[Catalogued as Letter 23]

[April 1872]

My dearest John,

I have been to Pescadero, picked up pebbles, and dabbled in the Pacific. You know how this has been the great object of my wishes for the last three years. The pebbles are really very pretty—not topaz and emerald as I rather expected, but various semi-opaque stones, and a few clear ones—mostly white or green, but other colours mixed up.

Miss MacCann and her brother and I went down by rail to Watsonville, where I made my first experience of a mudwagon[24] in the drive over to Santa Cruz. It began with being 14 miles, but gradually increased until it ended in 20. The road was pretty good for California, and we were packed so tight inside that we did not bump very much, nor was it very cold. Santa Cruz is not much of a town, but the country round is lovely. Cañons with clear running streams that never dry—and green hills with trees of various kinds, and especially redwood, and flowers— nemophila, eschscholzia, scarlet salvias, azaleas, yellow violets, oenothera, pink mallow, orange, columbine—and numbers of others.

The sands are very nice, hard and firm, few shells, but on the rocks, urchins and anemones—such large ones—one can drive along about a mile there—then the rocks shut it in—you see the high land at the other side of Monterey bay—and when Dr Hay drove us out on Monday, we went to another part of the coast about amongst some rocks, so like the Giant's Causeway, only instead of polygons, the rocks were all cracked up into squares, looking like a very bad attempt at pavement—as rough nearly as the causeway too, and running out into the sea, which came running up in great green and white waves—there was a seal swimming about there quite close to the rocks, and now I have seen a seal and a turkey buzzard, but not a bear or a rattlesnake.

We took one drive in a 2 horse rockaway[25] which was beautiful, up the country, through the river where the bridge had been broken down, and the ford nearly destroyed, and then over the hills, and down a cañon in a wood, a forest, with a road going down like this [sketch] the dark line is the road, which was deep mud, cut up into ruts and holes—so that a section would have been something like this—[sketch] we having to drive on the outer edge, as the real road was impossible—you may fancy how I held my breath till we were down. Then we had to get out, because we had to cross a grip like the letter V and then we came to a place which fairly posed our driver. He had asked a man how the road was to the big trees—and 'he guessed we might get along' but here it really was a question. It was a narrow track between a high steep bank, and a fence—and it had been worn into deep holes by a torrent, and partly filled up with loose rails—and then washed out again—however when we were all out, he did put the horses to it, and got over— one wheel being [sketch] up there and the other down at the bottom, indeed, as a rule I suppose where the horses can go, the carriage can follow.

The big trees, although nothing to the Calaveras,[26] are big enough for English eyes—one was hollowed out, and had been used as a house, by a family, and really was a good sized room. I found a great many plants and flowers and then we came away, and took the road again, in safety, and had a lovely drive through a forest, and along the side of the cañon, amongst trees such as I had never seen before. We went out once for a walk in a wood, Miss M. and another lady, when we were frightened by a huge dog, and so had to escape. He looked horridly fierce, but altho' he rushed out nearly a quarter of a mile to attack us, when he came close, I commanded him in a stern voice to go home, and he did, so I daresay our fear was unnecessary.

Mr M-C went back on Monday and we meant to go on to Pescadero, but the stage did not run until Tuesday, because it was Easter, so we had to wait. When we did go, we had such a load—9 inside—4 on the box, (only meant for a tight fit of 3), and one lying on the baggage behind—the rolling coaches don't run yet, and you know the Concords[27] have only the box seat outside, and as Miss M. always was eager to go out there, and indeed most people were too, I was generally inside amongst strangers—tho' once she was obliged to come in too. I daresay it was pleasanter for her than for me. The drive over to Pescadero was just as cold as could be, and we started at 8 and did not get in till 5—of course much of the way was bad travelling, and we had to go slowly, but a good deal was good enough, and then we went still slower because a certain Mrs Boston, 'a leading Church member at S. C.'—and I suppose a leading woman everywhere else too, from her manner, an old inhabitant of S. C., would keep on talking to the driver, and he turning to answer her, the horses walked. The most furious N. wind was blowing, and everybody was really frozen, except Mrs B.—who was draped in cloaks and furs and wrappers, and so did not mind, and she talked away, declaring we were 'quite comfortable,' when I am sure if her tongue had been as cold as my feet, she would not have said a word. However the journey ended in time, even tho' we did stop in the windiest corners, once that Mr Boston might inspect a railway, once that he and she might look at the new light-house. We dined on the road, at a funny old wooden house in a glen, the coast is exactly like the back of the I. of Man, and the road mostly runs along the open hillsides—about half is fine—the rest as dreary and monotonous as one can imagine.

The hotel at Pescadero was painting and papering, and full besides, and no fire when we went in—and the most miserable little poky rooms they offered us—one hardly large enough to get into. Then they proposed rooms in the empty hotel opposite, to which we agreed—and we went over there to sleep—such horrid hard beds, and a broken window, with the cold wind blowing in so. Tired and bruised as I was I could not sleep, and could get no warm water, because there was nobody in the house—however the thought of the beach kept me up. There was an earth-quake too, but I did not feel it, altho' I was awake a good deal of the night.

The stage was to go next day, but as there was a large party wanting to wait a day, and besides Wednesday's stage was all engaged, they had arranged matters for us, and we were sure of our day on the beach. Stages are mostly very accommodating we found. We were told the road up to San Mateo was dreadful, and dangerous from the mud, on Tuesday, but the coach went safely on Wednesday and it was sure to be better every day. *We* spent the whole day on the beach—having lunch sent down to us. The others, Bostons and Lyndes, and the minister went back to celebrate a funeral, which is a festivity Californians never miss apparently—but we felt no call that way, and waited down there till 4 o'clock, when the waggon which had taken us down came to carry us back. There was great excitement about the pebbles, and when we got back, they were all eager to know if Miss M. had found any nice ones—but I put mine in a bag, and said nothing, so I don't think anybody asked me, and I was too tired to scream about mine—I hope you will see them some day.

Next day we passed all the dangers of the road, and reached home safely, and I was glad to stretch myself on a bed which did not hurt or scratch me and sleep. I am very stiff and sore still—you know what Californian travelling is—and how near it goes to dislocating one's bones. I suppose we had about the best time—as there was not much mud, and little dust. *We* never stuck, and only once had to stop and help out a waggon. We had a beautiful day, and a *char à banc*[28] with 6 horses to Spanish Town. Then a mudwaggon again 6 horses to San Mateo. The road was perfectly lovely—most of the way—especially out of Half-moon Bay—where you ascend a capital road for 6 miles, and then find you are just over Spanish Town from which you started. I never care however to go to Pescadero again. I should like to see more of Santa Cruz, and to visit Monterey however. I have made one photograph frame with my pebbles already, and am going to make some more.

My dear, don't go and get out of spirits because business is not good—it will all come round in time. Just think of Edward's escape on the Harrisburg rail—when but for the snow drift he would have come in for the accident. You always are rather disposed to see difficulties. I have lived through so many, that I don't seem to mind them so much. I don't mean to find fault with you—but young people when they first begin housekeeping are of course not up to all the small economies and self-denials which are necessary. I know in *my* first year I spent £5 a week, when afterwards I made 3 do, when you two babies were to be provided for. That was in my prosperous days when I dressed well, and we gave dinner parties. I suppose if things are hard you will have to be economical in that way for a year or two. Small dinners run away with a great deal of money. If Edward prospers, we shall be able to help you—don't fancy I am pinched. I should like more because I should like to make you all presents and to help you along—but we can manage well enough.

Thank you for wishing me to come, but when you hear Edward's account of his journey you will understand how unsuitable it would have been for me—and the expense would be such an objection.

I have not *sent* you any sketches for I have made hardly any. I am always meaning, but have never done it.

I hope Mary has despatched my box of dresses, as they will take a long time coming, and I want them very much. If I don't get them soon, I shall have to buy something here which I want to avoid. I was in hopes the box would have started early in March—and cared more about that than about new patterns for the prints—but from her last letter I found she had not got them yet—which disappointed me. I am afraid I have given her a great deal of trouble and I am very much obliged to her for taking so much pains. I have only one decent dress to wear now—and so I shall be very glad of the others if I can get them before this is worn out.

I have sent some more small socks, and am going to knit larger ones next time. My best love to you all. Is not Edward improved—Goodbye,

Your affectionate Mother
Catherine A. Hubback

6

May 12th [187?]

Oakland

My dear John,

Your last letter ended with Edward starting for London, and we have had no further information of him except such 'cables' as Mr Makin may receive—by which I know he did get back to Liverpool. It upsets one's chronology sadly and deranges one's ideas when one has to carry on two series of dates—one by cables quite late, one by letter 3 weeks old. I don't think I like cables in consequence—they are like looking at the 3rd volume first,[29] or getting the story out of a newspaper review.

There is one thing I should be thankful to know however—when I am likely—if ever—to receive the dresses I asked to have sent to me. I wrote for them as I flatter myself so long ago that they might reach me at least by the beginning of May, but I might have spared myself the trouble apparently, and Mary that of buying them since the whole affair seems consigned to oblivion. If I had had the least idea that there would be such difficulty and delay in getting and sending them I certainly would have said nothing about it at all—but would either have bought what I wanted here, or done without and gone shabby and ragged as I have been obliged to do lately—and must do until I hear either that they are or are *not* coming, as I cannot afford to buy things in 'both' places at once. It seems odd to me that when I write for a thing you should suppose I don't want it, or at least that it does not matter when I get it. I wanted them as soon as they could be sent—as I always do when I ask for a thing. However I will be wiser in future, and if I send to

England at all it shall be straight to a shop with orders to pack up and send off what I want at once. I daresay you think me very cross about it—but I have waited patiently, hoping every week since the beginning of February that I should hear they were coming, and now I conclude as no more is said, that you mean to send them by Edward—and meanwhile I have hardly a dress to wear, fit to go over to the city or to pay a visit—and I think you would mind it if you were obliged to go ragged. There now, I have had my grumble, and will take up another supply of patience, and see what comes. I wonder however that Edward did not tell you how much I wanted the things, and hurry the box off.

There's been a French fair '*Pour la Patrie*'[30] going on here, to help pay the ransom, and as Miss MacCann had tickets given her, we went together yesterday the last day: the time to go to be fashionable is the evening, but that does not suit us—so we went about 12—when at first there was nobody there, and we sat on a bench and conversed as comfortably and more privately than in her room.

She and I agree pretty well in our view of Californian character—so does Mr Hassell—that the women here are all gossipping, scandal-loving, ill-natured smiling hypocrites, not one of whom can one believe nor trust. I suppose wherever people live in the public way which comes from boarding-houses, and excessive intimacy running in and out of each other's houses, and having no serious occupation except going to fairs, lunches and so forth it always will end in private squabbles, and back-biting—jealousies and feuds. I don't know what I should do if Miss MacCann went home, it is such a comfort to have one English friend on whose word one can rely—and all the others who lived close are gone—Mrs Wedderspoon, Mrs Hudson, Mrs Emerson, who were my nearest neighbours.

Robert Beagley arrived at the city last night, we presume, as his name was amongst the passengers. I suppose we shall see or hear something of him tomorrow. I desired Mr Holderness to bring him over here as soon as he could—and I will, if he likes, introduce him to the Kirkhams, and the Aldens—which is the best I can do for him. Mr Holderness himself has so cut himself off from all society in Oakland, that *he* cannot introduce him anywhere here, and I don't think much of his clique at Alameda where only he goes. Mr Wedderspoon would be more to the purpose, and Bob had better get introduced to him.

There's a French frigate here now, and there's a German one expected, when the Germans are going to get up great rejoicings and demonstrations, and triumphs over their conquered enemies, in the most approved way of Xtian charity.

The Roman Cs have built a very grand (wooden) cathedral here—and they are going to have a great fair and lottery there in it to pay for it, before it is consecrated of course—it is quite an ornamental building, with two high towers, and a very high roof—much the most conspicuous building in Oakland.[31]

The Romanists must be prospering boldly in England when Dr Goss can dare to say that the Church will never be free until the Sovereign and the Premier are free to profess their faith. Whatever they may come to do in England, at least in America one will be safe from being burnt as a heretic, so I shall stay here when you have cardinals for Chancellors and Inquisitors for judges, and all those who have been playing with popery so long will find it necessary to take to it in earnest.—Well goodbye,

Your affectionate Mother
Catherine A. Hubback

[postscript] I have not written to Edward

7

June 2nd [1872]

My dear Mary,

Before this reaches you, I suppose Edward will have left you—and will be on his way home. I am looking forward to that, as you may suppose, and wishing he would have been here on the 4th, when we have one of our few holidays.

Mr Holderness has gone with some friends to Yosemite, or as far as he can get towards it, as his time is short, and I have been alone entirely for two days. However as I had an empty room till Wednesday, I have absolutely volunteered to take in for those 2 nights a total stranger, whose name I don't yet know, nor whether he will be old or young, tall or short, pleasant or grumpy—and, oh dear, I quite forgot, perhaps he may chew tobacco, and *spit*!—and I have not such a thing in the house as one of those nasty spittoons, which are the usual ornament of American houses—drawing rooms especially.

But you will wonder how it happens that a stranger should be coming here. Well it is the clerical convention for this district, on Monday and Tuesday, and Mr Akerly announced in Church today that anyone who was disposed to take in a minister should signify it to him after Service. So it struck me that there was my room empty and not only a much bigger piece of beef than I wanted, but a crab ordered for Monday, before I knew H. H. was going to Yosemite, and it was evidently my duty to receive one of these strangers—I quite forgot tobacco and spittoons—and now I must take the chance. He is to come tomorrow—and I wonder whether he will be very hungry—H. H. is particularly partial to crab and salad—and I cannot often get a crab.

I did not know he was going until about 4 o'clock on Friday when he ran in, to get a pair of socks and a comb, (I advised a toothbrush also) and then ran off again, and taking the latch key, I believe—certainly leaving his whole room littered with clothes which I put away. I daresay my strange clergyman will not be very disagreeable—but it is a risk. That's the American way—I don't know whether anybody else, except for General Kirkham, offered to receive one—I think *he* did.

I hope, my dear Mary, you did not think I meant to accuse you of extravagance in housekeeping—I only think I believe you will find with experience that you improve, and that three years hence you will probably agree with me that the beginning is always the worst, and the 1st year the most expensive. I am glad you are not inclined to over-anxiety about worldly matters—some people are miserable all their lives for fear of misfortunes which never come. My sister-in-law Mrs F. Austen is one of those who always expects the worst, and has suffered more from dread of fevers, accidents and ill luck than most people would do of a severe illness once a year. 'Live for today, tomorrow's light, Tomorrow's cares will bring to light, Go sleep like closing flowers at night, and Heaven your morn will bless.'

H. H. tells me the box will arrive here about the 18th and he will get it through the custom-house. I have no doubt of liking the contents, especially with the guarantee of Edward's approval, and I am very much obliged to you for the trouble you have taken about them. I am afraid I have bothered you very much, and been very impatient for them—you will think, but I want the dresses really having reduced my wardrobe 'to the lowest span'—and have been uncertain what to do meanwhile. Things do wear out here—things that are washed wear out. What is not washed turns into tinder in hot sun,

I think—for alpaca which costs $2½ a yard—that is ten shillings English money, is worse—so tender in a few months that it tears on the smallest provocation, whilst I have had English ones which lasted years—and my last year's parasol is splitting both inside and out.

I have not seen much of our new neighbours. Mrs Jordan has the brusque unfinished ways of most Americans, who are either extremely affected, or unpleasantly natural—and the wrong side of easy—and I don't think you would much like your little daughter when she is 7 years old to be lolling round your neighbour's gates, and dawdling about on the streets as her children are in very dirty pinafores, and rough heads.

Parents here send their children to Sunday school to get religious teaching, and then wonder they know nothing, having trusted to the chance of teachers instructing them—and never seeing that they learn anything at home. But I think I have stirred up some of the boys I teach to care a little and take some interest, and hope in time to make my class (who vary from 9 to 12 years old) able to repeat the 10 Commandments accurately—of course they are all *gentlemen's* sons, and maybe future Presidents, so it is as well they should know the Commandments.

Goodbye, my love to John

Your affectionate Mother-in-law
Catherine A. Hubback

8

June 23rd [1872]
Oakland

My dear Mary,

I had a letter from you and one from Edward last week, which brought us down to their starting for London. I shall be glad to hear how they got on there. I heard also from Charlie last week, who has more difficulty now in finding time to write and means to post his letters than formerly. It seems he will be obliged to leave the mill, and I am anxious about what they will do. For my part, I wish they were here, as I think we could manage all together, and it makes me uneasy to think of the possible chances of Bernhardine being ill with no one to nurse her. However I suppose it is no use worrying. The last news of Edward was that he would leave on the 2nd of next month. I hope he will be able to do so—then he might be here in a month from this time.

My diversions last week were going out with the Akerlys, the whole family to a sort of country inn on the San Pablo road, and from there going down on the beach of the Bay. I went in a waggon with 6 of the children, four Akerly boys and one girl, and a boy who drove, name unknown, and Mr Bowen, owner of the waggon and inn. The others were in a basket carriage, borrowed—the Bowens gave us an enormous luncheon— boiled fowl, pork and cabbage, roast beef, vegetables, cherries, jam, rice-pudding, and for fear there should be nothing I could eat, she sent a special deputation to me to know if I liked eggs for luncheon—and *I* had a dish of poached eggs extra. There are sands on that part of the Bay, and we drove down and picked up agate pebbles, and petrified wood there—but this coast is very bare of shells, the ocean is too rough.

The weather had been cold up to last Monday, but that afternoon it changed, and since has been unusually hot, so that one could hardly move, and even sitting still, the heat was so great indoors that one had to be always *mopping* one's face. One hot day my neighbour's little girl had a bad fall sliding down the banisters, and broke her arm, close to the shoulder. Mrs Jordan called me in to comfort her, and when the doctor came, she asked me to stay with her—as she had not nerve to help him—so I had a lesson in applying chloroform, and setting an arm. It was broken in a very bad place, and there is danger she may have a stiff shoulder for life—she will be obliged to have it tied up for 30 days. She is only 6 years old, and this is the second bad accident she has had, as once 2 years ago she pulled over a marble-topped table on her chest, and was nearly killed, being insensible for hours, and ill for months. But when I told Mrs Jordan the other day that I was afraid her little girl would fall out of a window, she quite composedly said her children did not fall. I don't know whether they are Jews, but they are Jewish-looking, and have very large dark eyes, all of them—there are 4 children, of whom Constance the broken one is the eldest.

I met a Jewish lady and her daughter there yesterday, by name [failed to decipher], who had the keenest appreciation of my point lace work of anybody I have seen here. 'It was the most beautiful, elegant, valuable work!'— as to the value, they were sharp enough too, for when I told them I had worked a shawl, she priced it immediately, San Francisco price, just double what it would have been in England—oh yes she knew, she had asked the price—'Such work could only come from English hands—Americans could not do it!'

There was a young woman who came to Mrs Akerly to ask for a situation, as *she* wanted a girl to look after the baby—and amongst other questions the girl asked, what time did the baby go to bed, as she should expect to go out then, but she would try to come home soon after 10 if she could—also what room could she have to receive her visitors, as she had been used to have the use of a parlour—there being one young man who visited her regularly, and two or three who came at uncertain intervals—don't you think you would like such a girl as nurse? Sometimes they ask for the use of a piano, and sometimes require a horse and saddle—one could not engage where the rooms were not laid with Brussels-carpets—and they expect of course to take their meals with the family. In this country of happy equality young women consider domestic service a disgrace, and contrive to make it such a grievance and mortification to their employers that were it not for China boys I don't know what we should do—do our own work I suppose—which is not so bad where there are two or three women to help—but comes uncomfortable on one, who has not been used to it. But at present there is no lack of Chinese—as they come over in shiploads.

I have at last made acquaintance with one lady who understands botany, and is as enthusiastic about it, as I am; and a great deal more learned. She is the wife of Professor Kerr,[32] and lives in Oakland at present—tho' the University[33] will be soon moved to a place a good way off, and then I suppose all the Professors and their wives will go too. She is a very excitable lively woman, and we were friends directly. I shall tell her some day my genealogy and ask her if she knows the name of Austen.

Your little girl must be very forward for a first child, as they don't usually talk so early—Mrs Jordan's youngest, who is about the same age, says a few words, but then she has the other children to make her talk. Is it not pretty to see her walking about pushing a chair? John used to do that—I don't think Edward did.

The last Panama mail did not bring the boxes, so we hope the next will. Mr Holderness is as anxious for his, as I am for mine.

Mr Hassell and his friend enjoyed their visit to the Geysers exceedingly—only the snakes disturbed them. They killed one rattlesnake, and he brought away his rattle. I was telling Constance Jordan a story yesterday, and she was so surprised to hear there were no wolves or bears in England.

With love to you all

Believe me

Your affectionate Mother-in-law

Catherine A. Hubback

July 14th [1872]

My dearest John,

I daresay you have discovered by this time that you sent me a letter from Mary, instead of the one you intended, and which perhaps may come in another letter. I am sorry for Mrs Herbert's illness, but perhaps so far as the children are concerned, it is as well they should have no more.

I shall be very glad to hear that your wife and daughter are returned to you. It is very magnanimous of you to give them up, as certainly it is requiring a good deal of a man to expect him to acknowledge that *any* one has a prior claim on his wife. I hope Caroline Ingram may not suffer so much as such invalides do sometimes, but I know it is not only a very painful but usually a very tedious complaint, and if Mary is to stay away from you until she recovers, I opine your separation is likely to be a long one. I don't like husbands and wives being parted if it can be helped. If it were for any definite time I should think less of it, however I shall hope to hear soon that Mary has been able to return to you.

I am happy to say that Mr Makin is much better, so much that Mrs Ross has been able to go down to Monterey for a week with her son—I have never seen Mr James Ross yet, nor his wife, and they are a sort of myth to me.

Mr Higgins called yesterday and sat sometime. He had sent the ribbands the day before—they are very nice, and just what I wanted. He was pleasant enough—he knew me from my likeness of you, and I guessed who he was from his voice which was as north-country as if he had not spent 30 years in Australia.

I have left off imagining that Edward is coming home, and tho' I hear he will start next Saturday I don't believe it in the least, and shall not until I hear he has really started.

I like to hear about the old people and places we used to know, and think it very gracious of Mrs [failed to decipher] to ask after me, though if I stay here two more years, I shall have a chance of seeing her quite as soon as I should do probably were I in England.

I am very sorry for Mrs Bradbourne's little boy, it will be a great grief if they lose him I should think—but they are both such delicate people themselves one cannot wonder that their children are unhealthy.

Mr Higgins told me he was much surprised at the change in manners amongst the young people of England, and the general 'fastness' of the young women. I suppose the pendulum will go back again someday as it always does, both in dress and manners, and when they are tired of frills and levity they will take to plain dresses and affected stiffness.

What will become of the next generation *here* one can hardly imagine. My school boys today, who last week told me 'their neighbour' meant one who lived next door, today remembered that it meant everyone 'except Chinese'— 'they being heathens,' and 'coming here and taking the work from white men.' You may guess I gave them a sharp lecture—holding up the Chinese for filial duty &c &c—and saying it was no wonder when Christian! children set such bad example that they continued heathens still. How came California to belong to the U. S.?—I asked—and they said, 'We discovered it.'—No you did not—you coveted it, and came with an armed force, and stole it from the Spaniards, and drove them out.—The boy murmured something about the English wanting it—No, the Spaniards invited the English, but before they could answer the U. S. soldiers had taken it—but this is not in our lesson, except as an example of coveting and stealing. Do you suppose the U. S. fathers and mothers will raise a rebellion on account of my teaching such shocking truths? I suppose that the declaration that all men are born free and equal, means only all natives of the U. S. in their opinions.

The flies are horrid and interrupt me every moment by coming straight into one of my eyes, or lodging suddenly in my ear, which makes me jump. It is very warm also. I have been vaccinated twice, but it does not seem likely to come to any thing, so I shall let it be. The small-pox is not so bad as people say, and more people have died of sunstroke in New York, than small-pox here, or than have been sick of it here.

I am just beginning to revel in peaches and apricots, tomatoes, green corn, eggplant, and other luxuries. Not that we have got of the best—for the first apricots are always small and dry compared to what they will be in a week or two, and peaches are not so thoroughly ripe as they will be. We had a great many golden drop plums ripe, but so many were stolen that we had to gather them all—the other sorts are not ripe yet. There are cherries, raspberries, blackberries, pears, apples and grapes—also melons are just coming in besides several sorts of plums.

Mr Higgins promised to come over and see me again, but he has not—as he is to go on again on Wednesday next he will not have time to see much here, but he wants to make his son travel, and talks of coming out this way again with him.

They have succeeded in opening up a way from Yosemite into a valley beyond—I suppose they have made a road round the rocks which you said shut in the stream entirely- and they have found another finer and grander cañon than the first—but of course it is not very easy of access as yet, and one has to *rough* it a good deal. I wonder whether we shall ever accomplish the visit.

I can't bear these flies.

Goodbye

Your affectionate Mother
Catherine A. Hubback

~ 10 ~

My dearest John,

So Edward has really started, and must be now near New York—having been 8 days out. I don't think I can write sense today, as I have a head ache—there has been a sudden change of weather again. Yesterday the cold came to a climax, and I shivered in my Astrakhan—then for the first time within the memory of the oldest inhabitant (that's myself)—or at least for a fortnight we had a bright clear night, and a sunny morning— and I was too hot again, and woke with a consciousness of having a head.

However I got to school, and taught my boys, and so far interested them in the life of St Paul, that one boy asked me where he could find that story—was it in the Epistles? and I encouraged him to look it out and read it. I sometimes think that when the evenings grow dark so that they cannot play out of doors, I might get my boys to come up for an evening in the week, and give them a pleasure and do them a little good at the same time. You know they are not plough-boys—but more or less of gentlemen!—one is the clergyman's son. With the greater freedom of a room instead of a church, and books and maps to refer to, I think I might put something into them, which in the careful exclusion of all 'sectarian teaching' from their schools, they never learn there. I can teach boys I think, and on a weekday and out of church could teach with greater latitude in the way of nonsense or harmless fun, you know. I wonder whether it would do!

I am so glad Caroline Ingram has so far recovered—sometimes that complaint is tedious or incurable—but I suppose it depends on taking care at the beginning.

Miss Kirkham is to be married on the 22nd—and I have to work hard to get the lace finished which her mother bespoke. She runs in every now and then for an hour's chat, or rest, or change; she is very nice in a great many ways—she reminds me of Mrs Shanks—I think those wildish, odd people full of frolic and thoughtlessness, often take a fancy to me—I wonder whether it is a compliment—I am afraid not—rather the reverse perhaps. However it is pleasant in my old age to have young people taking pleasure in my society and not afraid of me. They have taken the house on 13th and Brush—which is just 2 blocks each way from us—I am so glad to have her near me. It will be a good thing for her to be married, people will leave off speaking illnatured scandal of her perhaps. Miss Woolsey asked me if she had not been engaged 5 or 6 times already, and would this come to anything now? However when she found they had taken a house, and ordered furniture and were making wedding clothes she began to believe.

In fact, Leila was really engaged before, but was obliged to break it off, last Spring, just after she came back from the Islands—because the family, especially the father Mr [failed to decipher] Marjoribanks opposed it decidedly—declaring he would disinherit his son—but she was very fond of him and felt it a great deal. She told me all about it and I think she was quite right and is doing much better now—as everybody thinks highly of Mr Blair, and young Marjoribanks was a great scamp, and not at all deserving her. Mr Blair knows it all—she is only 19, and I don't think much of the unconquerable attachments of girls of that age—so I expect when she has been married a year she will quite forget she ever did like any one else. It will be Mr Blair's fault if she does not.

Girls here come of age at 18, and can then marry whom they please, in spite of their parents' wishes—then they can easily get a divorce too—such is the charming state of society. I wonder what the next generation will be in America, or the next after that. Their only universal creed is that the Republic is morally, intellectually, physically and geographically the first country in the world, and that all the European communities are slaves governed by rotten thrones and bloated aristocracy. Their one universal creed is to get on—in any way—to make money is the business of men—to spend it that of women, and if they cannot make it—they make believe to make it, which often does as well, or better—because whilst there *are* definite limits to what is real, what is imaginary has no limit at all—credit especially—until it collapses. In this country so few people have a grandfather, that it is rather a marked thing to own one—and as to founding a family, such an idea is never thought of. Live for today is their motto, that those should *get* who have the power, and those should *spend* who can. Nobody likes to go to service, but they have to take to dress making, or clerkships or suchlike—they marry early, and turn into domestic drudges, making their own bread and dresses, and being their own servants, and working hard, and growing old early, and disappearing out of the world—and their children roll about in the streets and steal their neighbours' plums, and tear their own aprons, and get a good scolding for that—and grow up anyhow—to be worse than their mothers.

I told you I was stupid, and I have proved it by writing all this stupid nonsense—but I have done nothing at all this week but make lace, and heard nothing except the Jordan children squalling, and been alone mostly, as H. H. and everybody else is fearfully busy—working till 8—and not finishing then. Everybody is—and I suppose Edward will be when he comes home.

My love to Mary, and begging pardon for my stupidity

Believe me

Your affectionate Mother

Catherine A. Hubback

September 1872–April 1873

With financial help from his mother, Edward Hubback formed a partnership with Robert Makin, a young Englishman with similar ties to the Liverpool grain trade. From an office at 316 California Street, San Francisco, Makin & Hubback, commission merchants, brokered cargoes of wheat in a competitive environment. Catherine turned her attention to her youngest son, Charles, struggling in Virginia to support his family.

~ 11 ~

September 23rd [1872]
Oakland

My dearest John,

I was very glad to hear from you, and always am, but do not suppose I want to tax your few moments of leisure so severely that you need ever occupy time or space in apologizing for silence. Since you wrote, I know you have been busier than ever on account of the bad harvest, the potatoe disease and other contingencies. This will have given you plenty to do—I hope Mr Thorniewell's health will allow him to return to help you. I daresay his ideas of necessaries and his wife's to differ from yours and Mary's—wealth is always comparative—like many other things.

It is good of you to want to help your brothers but they must fend for themselves so far as that goes—Edward will do very well—poor Charlie has a hard time of it, and feels very much

the disappointment of not having earned an independence. I
always expected he would lose at first, people almost always
do—first or last and it comes easier at first—he is not to
blame—all he wants is water and as that is in the Hands of
Providence, submission and patience are the only things under
the circumstances. It is a great comfort that he is not to blame
and a satisfaction that he *minds* it so much—I should be vexed
if he were indolent and indifferent—and I can help him at
present. Rain must come someday—it never was known I
suppose to cease to fall in an inhabited country, and with the
rain his troubles will in a measure cease.

Just after I finished my letter to Mary last Sunday, another
Chinaman came into the kitchen. I went out and ordered him
away, when Bohea said he would go too—so I said he might,
but I would not have other Chinamen here—Bohea had had
his wages paid, so he packed up his bundles and went off
before dinner—luckily dinner was cooked; and I had only to
dish up; which I did—but he had the consideration to send
his cousin Ong here, who had been within for a few days once
before—Ong came in time to wash the dishes, and I have kept
him since—he is a good boy *at present*, how soon he will spoil
there is no saying—he puts too much lard in his pastry, and I
must get that altered, but otherwise he cooks very well, and
boils mutton much better than Bohea did, because he knows it
should not boil fast. He always speaks of men as *Shes*—'Is she
coming?' he says as he looks out for Edward at six o'clock—the
change saves $4 a month, which I am glad of—as $12 is quite
enough for our place—Bohea may easily get $20. They give
$30 at Mills Institute[34] to a man for ironing—but that is really
hard work it is so hot.

We have not got much into the excitement of elections yet
but I suppose next month we shall have processions and bonfires

and rockets in abundance. I could not at first make out what the difference in parties was, but I have discovered now—all the R. C.s go with Greeley who they expect will favor them more than ever—the R. C.s are all Papists, all other denominations are national and American, but Romanists adhere to the Pope, and acknowledge no other head, so that their united influence is naturally dreaded by such few Americans as think at all or have any real patriotism. There is lots of talk and boast about the size and power of their country, but that mostly is only a phase of self-conceit. There are those however who can see the danger of a foreign influence. Dr Manning's notable scheme (at least so Americans say) is expected to be much forwarded by Greeley's election.[35] It may not be a correct version, but the Irish American papistical scheme, under his name, is that France should rise to inaugurate a new crusade to restore Italy to the Pope, and give him back his Roman Empire. The French fleets could ravage the coasts of Italy whilst their armies defeated the Germans, Austrians and all other *heretical* states, especially with the help of America and Ireland in the destruction of all opposing powers, and the universal establishment of the power of Pio Nono[36]—and the triumph of the Romish Church. If Dr Manning[37] really imagined, published and advised any such plan he is a worse man by a long way than he was thirty years ago when he came to preach in our Church in Albany Street.[38] But I can hardly believe he would form a scheme worthy of Catherine de Medici for wickedness, and more foolish even than wicked. Harper[39] is my authority, and one cannot much trust American papers. The settlement of the Alabama claims will have one result at least – the Yankees cannot now carry out their threat of fitting out privateers in any future wars—and retaliating on us for the injury their own country-men did them.[40]

I have lost all faith in any proposals of Mr Heath, who has always been misleading us as to what could be done about my money. But as things now stand I am not sorry that it cannot be had at present. I don't want any more lost. As to his plan of Charlie borrowing the whole on mortgage I never would agree to that—and I told Charlie not to think of it. His own share, if by and bye he returned to England he might have, but not yours—it would end in some alienation or quarrel between you, and I could not die easily, if I thought such a thing possible. You see when after our death, your share came into your own possession, and it was locked up in some mortgage of Charlie's, either you and Edward would have to sacrifice or he would—no, if you want to keep friends as your uncle Herbert once told Mr Purvis—'I will sooner give you £10 than lend you £30'—so he was not asked again. Almost all family quarrels originate in money transactions, and if I lived my life over again, I would never lend any to a brother-in-law.

I hope your cook does well—I wonder if she would like to send up such a breakfast as Ong did this morning at 8:30—namely hot rolls, beefsteak, tomatoes, corn and an omelette. I only ordered the steak and tomato sauce—the rest was voluntary with him. My tomatoes are ripening finely, tho' they are rather backward because they have been too much shaded—another year I will try to tie them up—but it is not easy to get sticks here.

Mr Holderness when he left me, went to live at Alameda with two other young men, where they keep house together. Edward and I dined there one evening, and he drove us home—last week the 3 bachelors were a good deal astonished at 9 o'clock in the evening, of receiving a visit from 3 young ladies and 3 gentlemen, who rode over to spend the evening with them. The girls were Miss Woolsey and 2 Miss Rileys, the gentlemen's names I hardly know—one was Haven,[41] another one Colonel MacSomething. They have no connections, to each other, but all board at Kelsey house—and except Miss Woolsey were almost unknown to the 3 gentlemen of the house. Mr Holderness and Mr Platte were extremely annoyed—Mr Hall, who is a Southerner, thought it good fun. They pushed aside the tables, and danced, had coffee and stayed until eleven when they mounted and rode home. I suppose they would not reach home till midnight at least. Mr H. said that if he wanted Miss Woolsey to visit him he should have asked her father and mother too—as to the others he did not want them at all under any circumstances. Miss Woolsey was the girl who they tried to persuade Edward and me he was in love with—had he been, I think this would have cured him. By the way, one Miss Riley and the Colonel had paid them a visit the night before, when they stayed an hour, and drank whiskey and water. Mr Hall had been introduced to her at some party once—I suppose these are California manners—and the result of boarding house living—can you imagine how young women can make themselves so cheap? They should hear what the young men said of the intrusion.

There—I have written you a long gossip—I gathered my 7th and 8th lily today—Japan liliums—spotted and sweet and 6 inches across from tip to tip.

Love to you all, including my grandchild and
Believe me

Your affectionate Mother
Catherine A. Hubback

[postscript] We have got the church Hymnal at last, and been invited to join in the singing.

October 6th [1872]
Oakland

My dear John,

I suppose by this time you are come back from your wanderings in France, I suppose your brother-in-law also is married and you are returned home. I suppose we shall have no letter this week, as Mary's last was written on the eve of starting. I was so glad that Mrs Segar was to have your baby, I was feeling as if I ought to be there to do the duty of grandmama, and take care of the 'young ones' whenever they are in the way. That is what grandmamas are good for. I daresay the little lady got famously petted at Huyton, and the change of air I hope did her good. Ditto for you—I trust you enjoyed your trip very much.

I received the gloves, which are very nice and soft kid—I shall look for the others in time. Good gloves are dreadfully expensive here. I am glad Mary has done some work for Bernhardine. I have sent her some little things too, embroideries, and mean to supply her with socks as they are wanted. I can only send by post—as railroad charges are so enormous across the continent. I have not heard from them for a fortnight—then Charlie wrote dreadfully discouraged by the continued drought which has nearly ruined everybody. I tell him it *must* end at last—I am afraid they have a good deal of privation—and I never sit down to dinner without longing to impart some of our roast beef or mutton to them.

Edward says he thinks probably Charlie had better come here next year; and I do long for him more than I can tell.

We could manage for them well enough and if he did not—as I think he had better do—learn business, and help Edward when Mr Makin is gone, he might find something else—but my wish is that he should work with Edward—it would be a comfort to Edward himself if he had a brother to talk to and trust, as the responsibility will all fall on him when the Makins go to Europe next spring. This is their plan, and they will likely be absent a year. The business has prospered wonderfully, tho' Edward complains it occupies his thoughts too much—that he is growing dreadfully American and caring for nothing but money.

He is gone to Church this evening without me, for what with the heat and the long Service this morning I really did not feel equal to going again. You see if one goes to school at 10, and has an hour there before Church, and then attends the whole service afterwards, and does not get back till past one it makes rather hard work in this hot weather. It has been very hot for some days, and the mosquitoes are venomous—and as they have been (I don't mean mosquitoes) grading our street they have stirred up all the fleas, and aggravated them beyond their usual spite.

We have been reading Figuier's *Tomorrow of Death*.[42] I think if I went in for fancy sketches I would rather have Swedenborg's[43]— Figuier's are the most entirely fanciful and childish, so far as I have read of anything of the kind I ever came across.

They have got a fire engine here at last. We have not had any fires since it was bought. I am not sure whether there is any water to be had if wanted, even now—but they amuse themselves every now and then with ringing the fire bell at odd times, and making the brigade turn out. Once they rang it at 2 o'clock—which woke me— last night they rang it at 10—it is only a joke however. There has been no fire for sometime.

I rather expect an earthquake next. We are coming to the earthquake time—and it is as hot as it was the year you were here—and as dry as it ever can be—however my garden flourishes. I generally go out directly after breakfast and garden for an hour or more, when it is cool, and the air so delicious. Then if I have to go to market I tidy myself and go about 9—order meat, buy fish and fruit, etc.—and come home and sit down and cool—very often Mrs Blair comes in—about once a week at least, and sits an hour or more with me, to consult over housekeeping matters—or I go down to her after luncheon and pay her a visit. If I stay at home all the afternoon as I do when it is hot, I usually take a nap on the sofa—for half an hour. About twice a week Edward has to stay late, and then I have rather a long day. There will be 2 holidays next month, the election and Thanksgiving, when I hope we shall do something pleasant. The Makins are in town, so we may manage to join. They are come in for the winter. I hope you have been prospering too.

Goodbye

Love to Mary

Your affectionate Mother

Catherine A. Hubback

~ 13 ~

November 17th [1872]
Oakland

My dear Mary,

I have had a letter both from you and John since I wrote last; I was glad John was able to give a better account of little Carrie, I remember Edward had an attack of spasmodic croup when he was a baby. He could not lie down and I had to sit up with him all night—that is I sat up in bed myself holding him so that he should not choke with coughing. It is much better to keep children warm with clothing than with fires—because they carry the heat about them then instead of leaving it suddenly—and children are so impatient generally of unnecessary heat, that they never fail to complain of it when they can speak at all—and that I think is all one can judge by, as they are so different in their constitutions it is irrational to make one rule for a whole family. I know I used to suffer extremely from the cold when my brothers and sisters did not mind it—consequently I had dreadful chilblains on my feet and hands, which used to torment me all the winter. I scarcely had them at all on my hands after I was considered old enough to wear long sleeves—about 13 I think—and boots out of doors helped to cure my feet. Of course, had the same precautions been adopted earlier, I should have suffered less, but it was not the way!

I hope you had 'a good time' at Huyton and that Mr Segar was well enough to enjoy himself too.

I suppose Charlie has written before this about his vineyard as well as his son. They *have* had very hard times poor children,

worked hard, and fared hard. Bernhardine told me they had
sometimes nothing to eat and drink but bread and water. Fresh
meat they seldom see there, but they hope to get some at Xmas,
as they did last year. Want of water caused want of work, and
there was the rent to pay, altho' it brought nothing. Of course
nobody could have foreseen such a winter and summer—and
everybody suffered more or less. They did not complain or ask
for help as long as they could possibly avoid it—they have a
cow now, so I hope Bernhardine has the comfort of milk. At the
vineyard they will have a house rent free, keep for their cow, a
good garden and firewood—and a share in the profits—which
they expect will be more than last year as the vines are young.
Besides there will not be any night work—or any hard work—
and a good deal of leisure at times, which I hope that Charlie
will turn to some profit, either by his skill in mechanics or in
some other way. Their house is about a mile from Haymarket,
near the station and within reach of the Church—and there is
another near it, and a farm-yard opposite. The road is close to
it, but it stands high. Edward saw it when he was there, which is
how I know so much about it. The river was full when Charlie
wrote last, and he was busy carding wool, so he had not much
time to spare. I daresay Dina will write as soon as she can.

I had a letter from Miss [failed to decipher] last week, she
said she had never been in Liverpool since I left England, or
she would have called on you. Her brother called lately but you
were away—in France I daresay. I suppose you are having rain
and wind and storms and mud.

We had rain last week which set the grass growing and there
is a prospect of more. It is warm still, and cloudy. The Australian
trees are all coming out early. The *wattles*[44] as they call them are
almost blown. They are that kind of flower which we saw at
Johnson's when you and I went for flowers for your hair, and

he gave you bunches of little green buds. The blossoms are little feathery yellow balls, and so sweet. They cover the trees, and look as yellow as laburnums in spring, only not quite so bright. The arums too are beginning to put out flowers. I have some fullblown now in the garden. My first chickens did pretty well but were not so fat as I expected. I don't think Ong was careful enough about feeding them. I have another pair now, and I look after them more myself. I always feed my pigeons—but they are very shy. They coo now and I suppose will breed soon—but they will all crowd into one box.

John should read the Duke of Argyll's *Reign of Law*.[45]

Goodbye

Your affectionate Mother-in-law

Catherine A. Hubback

[postscript] I have had 3 pairs of short gloves and 2 long I think.

Oakland December 1st
1872

My dear John,

I suppose the time will soon come when our letters will get blocked in the snow, and we shall be two or three weeks without hearing of one another. There has already been a small block, and our rains have begun—last week it was very cold with frosts—quite sharp ones, which mashed up the tomatoe plants, and sent the heliotropes into half mourning. They were so beautiful before that—and I am not sure whether the frost has nipped the leaves of one abutilon or a gopher has gnawed its root—the poor thing looks badly anyhow, but if it is frost it will recover I think. However the frost is gone now, and on Friday morning more than two inches of rain fell in 24 hours, with thunder and lightning, and the wind all the wrong way, and a high barometer, which I am told indicate a probably wet winter. It has begun a fortnight earlier than last year. Here, as you know, the rain is a subject of the greatest importance to the country, and although after last year's abundance, we do not require a flood, still we need a proportion.

Just opposite our house on Grove Street is a depression in the ground, which gets full of water and does not easily run off. We used to call it Lake Emerson last year, in honour of our neighbours and landlord—but they are gone now, and the Jordans live in their house, so I call it the Dead Sea, because Mrs Jordan told me she was sure her little boy would run into it and be drowned! It is not likely to be deep enough to drown him really, and although it may make him muddy, it can hardly make him *dirtier* than his normal state, he being one of the grimiest children I ever saw.

I made a curious discovery the other day. Do you remember I used to know a Mr Hepburn at Malvern, whom I liked very much, and who was the original of Mr Hamilton in *Malvern*?[46] I learnt from Mr Blair accidentally that he came out here some years ago, and died the year before I left England. Mr Blair happened to mention the name, curiously enough in connection with one of our old jokes about the letter H. Mr Hepburn was talking of the little *Auk*, and some American lady observed 'How curious it is you Britishers never pronounce your H—I suppose you mean a *Hawk*!' I thought it was just what my Mr Hepburn would have talked about, and began asking about him, and we made out it was the same man, beyond all doubt, as he had part of his hand and little finger shot away, and I always saw him in a glove—besides being tall, handsome, rather awkward, very pleasant, a great naturalist &c &c &c. Mrs Blair told me since that her husband kept on reverting to the oddity of my having known him, and hearing of him out here—and for my part talking of him made me dream of old times again. I wish he had lived for me to see him again—but I am glad to know what became of him. You always used to say I never met anybody without finding out our spheres had some connecting link somewhere. The fact is the world is but a little place—but still I did not expect Mr Blair whom I did not know six months ago would have been able to tell me news of an old friend. Mr Blair himself must have been only a boy, when I knew Mr Hepburn 24 years ago. I see a good deal of Mrs Blair, and little bits of her husband, who comes in often before I leave her, especially when she is not well—she is very delicate, and apt to overtire herself. I never saw two people more in love, and with her it has come on since her marriage.

It is such a wet fog, and the roads so muddy that I did not go to Church this evening and Edward is gone alone. Besides I was rather tired, as I had school, and then the long service, it being Sunday for Communion. I have actually 12 scholars in my class now, though they do not usually all come: one has been sick of scarlet fever and away for many weeks though he is well enough to go out—but the others were there today—there are 3 joined quite lately. They volunteer to come. James Akerly is one of them—his younger brother has been in my class for a long time—and 2 brothers were introduced today by another boy. So far as I can see they come quite as they please—without any reference to anybody else—or I may say, any reverence for anything. I try hard to make mine steady, and I really believe have some influence on them, but the irrepressible republican nature, never checked or controlled so far as I know, is always bursting out—and it is terrible uphill work, though I should not like to give them up at all now. If it were anywhere but in a Church I would overlook a great deal of levity, but I feel responsible if I allow irreverence there—and yet—Edward says he never saw a worse behaved set, altogether than they are— not mine however in particular but the whole school—indeed it is absurd to call it a *school*—it is nothing but a fortuitous collection of boys and girls, who do just as they please, and spend most of their time in playing or chatting.

I have been reading an answer to J. S. Mill's book on the Subjection of Women.[47] American 'women's rights' women seem to me like the fisherman's wife who was not satisfied with anything short of the sun and moon. In this country they seem to me to have their own way from babyhood until they are mothers—then of course they have to take their turn at submitting to their daughters—but in public so far as the best places go, and in private in their own homes they rule, and the law allows them not only to hold property independent of their husbands, but to devise it to anyone they please *in spite of him*—whilst they have a share in all his, and he cannot leave it or settle it without his wife's consent. She has, in event of widow-hood, half of his real estate in fee-simple, all his personal property, and her rights of dower besides—and all her own if she has any—pretty well, I think. Widows here almost always remarry, sometimes more than once. I don't know how the money goes in divorces—perhaps they each keep their own. I do not think the morals of California have been making a brilliant figure in the world lately. Mrs Fair's murder trials and acquittal, the forgeries and escape of the Brothertons, and the great fraud about the diamond fields, have made more conspicuous than creditable figures. Mrs Fair is living in Oakland now, and the other day was in the same car or boat with the widow and daughter of the man she shot dead before their eyes—and was acquitted of murdering! It is not that people are not indignant—but what is the state of this country when money can procure such a verdict? The Brothertons indeed were speedily retaken—but money was the cause of their capture, as well as the means of their escape. So many had lost by their forgeries that public indignation compelled the officers to exert themselves and retake them. I don't pity the diamond speculators—and feel rather triumphant that the *Times* foretold the result.

I hope I shall have a letter this week. I heard from Mrs and Miss Lee last week.

Love to you both.

Your affectionate Mother
Catherine A. Hubback

~ 14.5 ~
[*Catalogued as Letter 19*]

Oakland
December 15th [1872]

My dear Mary,

Don't suppose that I am reduced to second childhood, and therefore obliged to rule my lines, but as Americans cannot write straight (or think they cannot) without lines, one cannot procure paper here which is not ruled. I hate it extremely, and if I had known, I would have brought out more paper when I came. I had yours of the 21st last night, with two delightful pairs of gloves—long ones and dark colored. I am glad of the dark at this time, and I expect one of them will last me all the winter.

It has been very cold for California, but dry and calm—so calm that windmills are no use, and have not worked for this month. People are prognosticating a violent storm. I suppose the rains will soon come but we have had enough to make the grass quite green.

Just at this time there has been more gaiety in Oakland, than for a long while, and I was actually out twice last week, one concert, and one evening party. Edward had 2 other dances, so he did pretty well. I fancy next week Oakland will burst out into Christmas trees. Everybody here declares she is as busy as possible working Xmas gifts. Our neighbour Mrs Jordan told me she had worked a dressing-gown for her father, quilted and wadded all thro'—a very pretty attention, and as he lives in Oregon, he wants a warm dressing-gown.

She and a tall friend made a descent on us on Tuesday evening, and sat sometime. Mrs Jordan wound a skein of red wool

19.

Oakland
Dec 15th 1873
[?, 1872]

My dear Mary,

Don't suppose that I am reduced to second childhood, and therefore obliged to rule my lines, but as Americans cannot write straight (or think they cannot) without lines, one cannot procure paper here which is not ruled — I hate it extremely, + if I had known, I would have brought out more paper when I came — I had yours of the 21st last night, with 2 delightful pairs of gloves — long ones + dark coloured — I am glad of the dark at this time, + I expect one of them will last me all the winter — It has been very cold for California, but dry + calm — so calm that windmills are no use, + have not worked for this month — People are prognosticating a violent storm — I suppose the rains will soon come — but we have had enough to make the grass quite green — Just at this time there has been more gaiety in Oakland, than for a long while, and I was actually out twice last week, one concert, + one evening party — Edio had 2 other dances, so he did pretty well — I fancy next week Oakland will burst out into Christmas Trees — Everybody

6 First page of Letter 19. (*MS. Eng. lett. e. 150, fol. 49*)

and sewed a few other things besides the dressing-gown, her friend did nothing, and said as little, except when I laboriously extracted some small sentence from her. As Mrs Jordan has 4 very noisy children I have no doubt she prefers a silent friend, but it is heavy work to imagine amusement for a person who sits up like one of the Needle-rocks, and lets your efforts die, like waves at her feet.

One of the Xmas trees on the eve is to be in the Church, for all the children of the parish, and we were all asked to subscribe for it today. I don't like using the Church for a Sunday school— but it goes beyond that rather to have it used for such a purpose. Edward and I are engaged to attend one down at Kelsey house the same evening, so we shall inevitably be absent from the church one, but I do not think I should have had anything to do with it had we not been: indeed I do not know the principal contrivers and abettors of this, and I don't attend the Associate Ladies' vestry meetings on Wednesdays, so I am not bound to know anything about it.

It was a very good concert that we went to—Spanish and German singers mostly, and only one American. I hate American women singers, they have all head and throat voices, are apt to sing through the nose, and scream shrilly. One of them tried to sing 'Casta Diva',[48] and of course failed, but the natives did not know it, and applauded her vociferously.

I did not know till I had a letter last week from Mrs Frank Austen that old Mrs Lefroy was dead. Mrs F. A. takes it for granted I knew it, and only alludes to it in a parenthetical way—nobody ever told me. I also infer that Mrs Knight of Chawton house is dead—as Fanny says she saw a memorial window to her—*that* I had not heard of otherwise. I do not get many letters from anybody but you and John. My sister has written once in the last year, and I hear about once in 3 months from Fanny Frank and Mrs Lee or Katie write pretty regularly. From the rest of my kin I have not heard a word for I don't know how long.

Since your letter was written, we hear that you have had most awful storms. I hope it did you no harm, and that John was not incommoded crossing, tho' perhaps he had to go to Woodside if it was very bad. I suppose we shall get some papers with the particulars. People exaggerate so here. Mr and Mrs Richardson, who left New York on Saturday week, must have caught it pretty badly on the Atlantic.

The new Mrs Wedderspoon is a person to whom I feel a strong attraction—she reminds me much of a very dear friend, Mrs Seymour of Porthview—who was also of a Scotch family—and I hope to be friendly with her. If so, it will be something to compensate for the loss of Miss MacCann with which I am threatened. *She* says she will go home next April— and I suppose she will, although at least *one* person wants very much to stop her. For my own sake I should like her to settle in this country—but as I told her, I would never *advise* anybody to marry—they must take the responsibility on themselves. As her home is in Birkenhead, I suppose you will see her and I shall envy her. I think very likely however you will not like her—we differ so very much usually in our appreciation of people in general. I suppose we shall not see Hal Segar until Spring. I hope he will find time to call on us, and not do as young Beagley did.

My love to you both and Goodbye

Your affectionate Mother-in-law
Catherine A. Hubback

~ 15 ~

My dearest John,

I am glad the letter came in good time with the bit of work. We had the MacCanns over here on your birthday to remember it. I suppose we shall soon get an account from you or the papers of the great storm you had, of which by telegraph we have something heard. I hope your windows were not blown in. I used to be afraid sometimes about those large heavy panes in the bedrooms.

We have had a severe and lengthened frost, for nearly 3 weeks, every night clear, starry, and freezing, every day bright, sunny, and hot—such blue skies, and utterly calm the whole time. Indeed there has not been wind enough to turn the mills for a month, and many houses have been seriously inconvenienced. The frost went on encreasing every night, and heliotropes and abutilons, and some geraniums have fallen victims to it. I don't know about my datura, it has been covered all the time, and perhaps may escape with its life, but it looks very poorly and thin now. So I have not much to boast of now of garden flowers. However my arums (callas or lilies they call them here) are blooming cheerfully, and don't look pinched. And today has been cloudy, and the frost has given, and whilst we were at Church it rained, and is raining now, so we may hope the cold is over, and that the wet season is begun. People of course had begun to get frightened, lest we should have a dry winter again: but it seemed to me quite premature to be uneasy: and I daresay we shall have enough to make us all tired of it before it is over.

Mr Akerly being ill it was announced that there would be no evening service, and as Edward has a cold, he will be just as well in the house, so we need not mind the rain. The wind too is getting up, and I expect we are really going to have *the* storm of the year which I have been told usually comes about Xmas.

Last Wednesday Edward and I engaged to go and dine in the city with Mrs Ross and the Makins, intending to come home by the 9 boat—but when I went over at one by appointment, having told Ong we should want no dinner, and not come home till late, Edward met me at the boat to say that he and Mr M. had to go and attend a grand dinner given to a man just going to Europe, and what would I do? It seemed there was no chance of the dinner being over even by 11, so it was finally settled, we should both sleep there, and they made us as comfortable as they could, but it was bitter cold, and I had no dressing-gown of course, and no hot water at night, and was very glad to come home next day. I never find any bed so comfortable as my own, go where I will, so I suppose it gets to fit me by habit.

On Friday evening we went down to celebrate Mrs Blair's birthday, by a little party. It was given on short notice, and a good many people could not come, or would not, so there were only 6 ladies in all, and a good many more gentlemen. In consequence we all had to dance, and to make up to Mrs Blair for her disappointment we all did our best, and I danced 3 quadrilles and Sir Roger—the first and last with Mr Blair, the Lancers with Mr Finney and one quadrille with Edward.[49] Mrs Blair declared it did her good to see me dancing, which I was glad of, for I am sure it did me none, although of course I was glad to oblige them—but it is too much for me; not but what I like it well enough. I did not wear my white Point and velvet, as I did once before, but trimmed myself with black lace, and wore an overskirt of black tulle and bugles,[50] over velvet, which made me look 'almost handsome' like Miss Squeers.[51]

We are moreover engaged to a party at Kelsey house for Christmas eve, but if it comes on wet, I don't much think I shall go, for though the cars might take one down they would not bring one back, and Oakland ways are too muddy to encounter when there has been 24 hours rain, on a dark night, which Friday will be.

I went on Wednesday before dinner with Mrs Makin to see some paintings exhibiting at the City. Some of them were very pretty French and German artists which were well worth looking at—and one which I thought was English scenery, as there was a large beech tree but it was New Hampshire instead of Old.

I heard from Charlie last week—they have got into their new house, where I hope they will be very comfortable, Edward says it is a very nice one. They will have poultry, and eggs and milk (for they have a cow) all great helps in housekeeping, and as they have two good pigs to kill they will also have a stock of bacon. Mr Wittichen is to pay them $12 a month for his board, which I suppose will find them in other necessaries until they receive something in the way of profits. Wood for fuel, house rent, garden and cow-keep are all part of the agreement—and corn or wheat at wholesale prices I think. I shall recommend Charlie to try and get work in mending machinery, as there must be leisure time, he will be close to a town and the Post Office—so that he will be able to receive and send letters regularly, also to go to Church. I knew the name they intended to give their child either boy or girl long ago. I hope to have another grand*son* in February—and fully expect they will find it all much better than the first time.

With love and best wishes to you both, believe me

Your affectionate Mother

Catherine A. Hubback

~ 16 ~

My dear Mary,

There were two mails came together last week and no letter from you, only one from Charlie. They had been stopped in the snow, at one time, but that would not account for there being none in either, so I suppose you have been busy someway.

I was very glad to hear of Edward Segar having entered the firm. It will be gain to John to have a junior partner to bully, and still more gain to have another share. I suppose Mr Makin will be off this week and then my Edward will be busy, but as he has been so all along I do not know whether it will make much difference. I hear from other people that the firm are supposed to be doing very well, and it is always an advantage to be *supposed* to be successful—and that Edward will be a very desirable *parti* for any young woman. I daresay—but I don't know the young woman *here* who would be so desirable for him.

We have just I think finished up another spell of wet—it rained violently last night, and it had been raining for nearly 10 days but the wind has gone round to northwest and it has cleared now again—but it was wetter this morning than ever I saw it. Indeed I believe the underground lake which I believe exists under Oakland is full to the top now, and we are almost floating, so that the water does not run away so fast as it did at first. The ground shakes so much more than it did a while ago, when trains or carriages go by. My theory of earth quakes is that they are caused by parts of this chasm falling in, and I rather expect we shall have a big one by and bye. There was one up at

San Leandro last week but they are much more frequent there than here, and it is said to be the real earth-quake centre.

My boy told me last week to get a new one, as he wanted to go, 'You get other boy tomorrow—I go away.' So I had to—and the only boy I could get is a man—Moon, he calls himself—who has a silk tassel to his hair, and he not only knows very little cooking, but still less English. It is not easy to get on with no language in common, as you say—it is a trial. I took him on trial—and I find him such. But today, as we came home from a walk I heard a great talking in the kitchen, and there was another man, who said he was Moon's brother, who said he 'had come from Samki—you savez Samki—he say that Moon go back to Samki—he no learn cook. I come here, I learn cook, my broder he go to city, he go to Samki.' Meanwhile, Moon's face assumed a look [sketch] like that— tho' that *is* flattering—and he said not a word. After a great deal of palaver and gibberish the other man was ejected, and Moon went and locked the door and then poured out a torrent of *pidgeon English* quite unintelligible—however when he had calmed a little, I made out that Samki wants him to make cigar boxes—'I no likee make boxes, I likee learn cook, I no go'—and he wants to stay here, but appears to be a good deal afraid that Samki and an unknown but overwhelming force of Chinamen will come whilst I am out, and carry him away. If they come when I am at home—I am to say to them 'Go long—get out—get out *dam smart.*' That's what they learn here. But of course I had to let it pass—how could I make him understand not to swear? Perhaps when we have more means of communication I may tell him *dam* is a bad word. It is an odd world, when one comes to think of it. When I was your age I had little idea I should ever be teaching cooking to a Chinaman in California.

I think this month is when you expect your confinement, I hope to hear it was over before you read this. *Je vous prie faites un garçon*—however if it is another girl, it can't be helped—but I expect it will be a boy. They were hoping to have the little Charles christened when Charlie wrote last—they are near a church now.

I have undertaken the management of the young ladies' association at earnest request, and they are to meet at my house. I would not do it if I had to run after them. There are to be 7 or 8 to begin, perhaps some more may join—and we settled they should begin by learning *guipure d'art*; and I shall set them all netting on Friday—it is a kind of work much sought here, and not much done, and as the work is to be sold it is well to do something salable. I thought it was best to settle on *all* doing one kind at a time, as it will be easier to teach.

I made a failure in an omelette this morning, the pan was not clean, and the fire was too blazy, so it burnt—which was unlucky—my breakfasts and dinners when I was sole cook

7 Examples of *guipure d'art* or *filet*, a simple form of darned lace which Catherine taught to the young women in her circle. (*Courtesy of Lacis Museum of Lace and Textiles, Berkeley*)

were generally very successful. Can you scramble eggs? John knows what scrambled eggs are.

I have had a bad cold and cough—everybody has—it is going away now, and if it keeps fine I shall soon get rid of it—but now I must go and see how the dinner gets on. I did, and succeeded in getting some good soup, and there was plenty of roast beef, which was lucky as Mr Warren came here, and dined with us. He was the clergyman I had last summer. I shall conclude now with love to you all.

Believe me

Your affectionate Mother-in-law
Catherine A. Hubback

White Sulphur Springs
April 27th [1873]

My dear John,

I had your letter with the very welcome news that the money was really paid, and that my forebodings had not been justified, last week, but it was before *that* that Edward had proposed to come up here, where the Blairs were staying; however we came with all the lighter heart, when we knew that money was secure, and that also we could reckon on another trip when Mr Makin returns. Edward must go back tomorrow but I am going to remain until Wednesday—Mr Blair goes backwards and forwards about 3 times a week.

We came up by the Vallejo boat leaving San Francisco at 4—and did not get here until it was quite dark so I saw nothing of the country from St Helena on the rail—or indeed from Napa—and less still from the stage up here. The valley is lovely and the flowers are so also. You know what California valleys are when they are full of trees, as this is. Edward and I have a little two rooms in a row of four dwellings—with a door outside each way, and neighbours on each side of us—there are other houses which stand alone with a sitting room and two bedrooms. There's a dining-room where we have our meals, and a ladies' room—they are all detached— and people come trooping in from all sides, when the gong sounds.

There are the most splendid butterflies here, and Edward says he saw a lovely humming-bird, but I have not seen it yet. The flowers are beautiful too—the scarlet larkspur which we

8 *At the White Sulphur Springs* by Carleton Watkins. Although this 1868 stereograph was taken five years before Catherine's visit, one can imagine her among the group of well-dressed people assembled at the entrance to the Napa Valley resort west of St Helena. (*Robert N. Dennis Collection of Stereoscopic Views, Miriam and Ira D. Wallach Division of Arts, Prints and Photographs, New York Public Library, Astor, Lenox and Tilden Foundations*)

found in a wood is particularly pretty, and the ground is as thick with white nemophilas as it would be with anemones in England. The water both tastes and smells filthy, and I am glad I am not obliged to drink it, as Mrs Blair's pug dog is.

I don't think you need pity me for any part of my Californian life, unless it is that stockings will wear out so fast and clothes cost so much. However [I] want Mary to send me out some new stockings as well as handkerchiefs by Mr Makin. Stockings at 2/6 a pair and her size would do as I know she can wear my boots. I like my stockings to fit and want 12 pair. You must repay yourself for both.

But to go back to my life—it certainly agrees with me, as I have grown stouter having gained 8 pounds in weight—and I would much rather teach a China boy than an English girl even or an Irish girl certainly—one never gets impertinence in words, and even if they are angry they only slam the door. They cannot speak well enough to be saucy. I have had to change 3 times lately, and I sent the last away before coming up here. He knows so little English that I could not make him understand an abstract idea—he thought I was angry with him, and said pathetically—'Me go—you no likey Wan'— with his hand on his heart and his diagonal eyes blinking narrowly. He is to come back Wednesday—we only came to terms through an interpreter. The scene between them was comical. The wash boy who interpreted is very handsome— like a Hindoo I think. [sketch] Mine—'Wan' is not beautiful, as you may guess—he say 'Lon man tin shon ling mann kin wa'—the other 'Wa kin mann ling shon tin man lon'—then the interpreter says perhaps 3 or 4 lines of blank verse of the same style and always in a chant, a gregorian I believe—and like a French tragedy—if one says two syllables the other answers with 5 or 6 so as to fill up the cadence.

I made up that thistle gown which Mary chose last year to wear here—it is very pretty. I like to hear about Carrie and baby—you need not be afraid of tiring me. I do not feel much inclined for letter-writing today what with the flowers, butterflies and birds—the blue jays are so beautiful and bold.

Goodbye.

Love to you both

Your affectionate Mother
Catherine A. Hubback

October 1873–July 1874

The letters resume after a six-month gap. The Hubbacks have been displaced at 11th and Grove Streets by their former next-door neighbours: the landlord's brother, Ralph Emerson, and his wife. They have taken a house in a less desirable location near the Central Pacific railway embankment at 959 7th Street.

~ 18 ~

October 11th [1873]
Oakland

My dear John,

I had a charming long letter from you last week which entitles you to another today but I wrote to you last week also. I said nothing to Edward about the money you mentioned, but he had before said he should be very glad at such a loan, and if you can manage it without inconvenience it will be a great help to him. Of course he would pay interest for it, and here 8% is not high interest for money, sometimes one gets 10 or 12—and it could be secured to you eventually on his share, so there would be no risk to you, and more profit on the money than you could get in England. I should be glad in every way if you could do it. Edward has about that much money of mine in use now, but if he had yours, I could help Charlie along.

I hope the latter is settled for the winter. I do so wish he could get regular business as an engineer or mechanical workman—he could combine it with a chicken ranch if he had the latter, and it would be much better than ploughing or wood chopping. I rather hope his engagement this winter may lead to more work of the kind. I do not know whether we shall be able to see him on our way out, but I hope so, as we could then talk over everything, and we should see how he had got through the winter.

Edward has not started for Oregon yet, he told me yesterday it depended upon the arrival of a ship at Portland which he was to meet, so he cannot tell exactly when it will be. We contemplate starting for England, if all is well, next February if the roads are open—which most likely they will not be, and we shall have to wait I expect a week or two or three after everything is fixed.

This will break up our young ladies' association—I expect. At least I don't know whether there is anybody likely to take my place. So few Americans know anything about fancy-work or needlework of any kind except making dresses, which they can do mostly more or less. They have no time for anything also, because, you see, driving round to see their friends and lunch with them, and going to all the funerals and weddings and receptions, and such, festivals and dancing, etc. etc., [they] have no time for anything else except a novel now and then. Do women really wear the enormous ruffs and fans that *Punch*[52] represents in England? They do here sometimes—I have not adopted them yet.

General Kirkham and his family are going to Europe next spring for a two years absence. May Kirkham is delighted at the idea—she has never been in Europe, I think. They talk of England—so perhaps we may see them there—but I do not think she would be dangerous there. I don't believe Edward has at present any serious idea about her—she is one of the very few young ladies he knows—and I do not think she cares for him at all more than for any other young man. She likes flirting a little as most girls do—but she is too young to marry now—and he had much better wait, and realise a position. I have no particular objection to May, except that I do not think her good-tempered, and she is used to having everything she wants—but I would much rather Edward should marry an English girl—a well-educated English girl has so many more occupations and ideas than any American I ever saw, that even if she does not dance quite so well, I think she would make a better wife.

I hope your concerts will be a success, and that you will enjoy your lessons.

I have made up the blue merino, and wore it yesterday, it looks very well—but I abjure flowers in a heavy material, so that my labours in dress making are not so severe as those who have to make [failed to decipher] out of a skirt.

We have had no earthquakes to speak of yet—the weather is very hot now but clear and delightful, as it rained hard nearly all last Wednesday, and it had been showering the day before—it freshened everything up extremely.

My new garden is really flourishing beautifully. I have had the first crop of weeds all removed, and now I hope there will not be so many—it was the largest charlock I ever saw. Our house is very comfortable especially my sitting room which has a charming bay window looking west. It makes a delightful room at this time of year as our drawing room is north. I am going to have a Chinese sofa in it, the *sitting* room—then it will be all complete—it is matted, and has a large table covered with a painted cloth, so that I can *cut out* on it.

I like to hear all about the babies very much. Love to you all.

Your affectionate Mother
Catherine A. Hubback

[NOTE: Letter catalogued as number 19 has been moved to Letter 14.5]

January 4th
1874

My dear John,

I am sorry you have been disappointed about letters, I know I did not write one week, we were in such uncertainty and trouble, it seemed no use, as I could only say what I might have, and should have had to contradict immediately.

When Mr Makin really started I felt quite sure that we were not going—but for several weeks—it seems to me months the time was so long—I was quite expecting to be *now* at New York. I am glad we had not to be so. It would have been a great loss to us in every way, and the worry and trouble—oh dear—I don't know if I should have got through it. I am well enough—only anxious days have brought back the old pain in my heart, which I used to have when you were only a small boy. I daresay it will go away again. It is not so bad as it used to be 25 years ago—only reminds me of old times.

As to Edward's business matters, he must explain those himself—but I can assure you, *he* is not blamed in San Francisco for anything that has happened. On the contrary, everybody (except Mr Makin) is quite sure he did right—and also quite aware that he did everything that could be done to set Makin straight. How he suffered nobody knows—but he used to be so worn out that twice he dropped asleep in the cars coming home, and woke up at Alameda. But for him in fact no final arrangement would have been made, as nobody likes Mr Makin well enough to trouble themselves to help him—certainly not Mr Blair. People at Liverpool must be very sure they are

immaculate, or they would not go and blame him to you. Yet I
have heard of some Liverpool men failing too. However people
who fail dishonorably and try to cheat their auditors, and keep
their money in some other name, tend of course to suppose
other people to do the same. When Mr Makin comes back, I
suppose Edward will go to England—perhaps that may be in
May or June. I expect Mrs Ross and Mrs Makin will want to
come home in the Spring.

We have not as yet had an answer from Charlie to my
proposal that he should move here this month. I wrote on the
13th and we ought to have a reply now. They mean to call the
little girl Catherine—perhaps Bernhardine also—but were
not quite sure. Dina had got quite strong and well, but he last
wrote they were in much perplexity about what they should
do as they would have to leave their house and could not find
anything to do, and thought we were going to England. It is
for their sake greatly that I am so glad we are not going—as
we can receive and settle them. I wrote to you last week all
particulars as to my plan for them which I also have detailed
to Charlie. I am very anxious to hear from him, my only doubt
being that when he thought we could not help him he might
have made some other arrangement. I believe Mr Wittichen
would not object to helping him on the same terms, but
Charlie thinks them much too bad besides that Mr W. himself
is not a pleasant person to be under. If he comes here he will
be his own master if my plans can be carried out.

Another reason why I don't want to leave just now is that
I have a pupil whom I like teaching, and having one may lead
to more—Adèle de Fremery the Dutch consul's daughter
comes to me once a week, and besides this even if I do not
get a class for teaching lace, as I am trying to do, I have many
orders for work, and last month I earned over 20 dollars which

I certainly should not expect to do in England. I like Adèle very much, and I know she likes coming to me, tho' her time is so taken up with masters that she can only come once a week. One does not lose *caste* here by teaching anything. That is one sensible thing, and people here who know me are willing enough to interest themselves for me I have given up the young ladies' association—I think I told you—and they gave me an elegant *souvenir* at Xmas.

New Year's Day was such a pouring wet one that nobody could pay any visits. Edward stayed home and read nearly all day. I meant to have gone to Church, but should have been wet through.

There's a young lady boarding at Planel House where Miss MacCann is who knows your uncle George and May and Roland's Caitte. She told me a lot about the people there. Is it not odd meeting people who know one's friends all round the world?

How much mischief was there done by your high tides? Was the esplanade at Rock Ferry washed away again? or any of the boats swamped? Edward saw something about it in the papers. Mrs Tom Wedderspoon knows Rock Ferry and Bebington Church, where the bells were rung for her brother Mr Jolly's wedding with a young lady there whose name I have forgotten about 3 years ago. She remembered Mr Williams too—I am very sorry for him—I think he had a young family—but he was only just come when I left.

We have had an immense deal of rain; if they wanted to sow rice on some of the streets it would be just ready for it—and only want harrowing over—Oakland was described accurately as waterlogged. I believe the great cave underneath is full, and till the water runs off we shall not get dry—but when it empties I daresay we shall have a pretty smart earthquake, as the roof will be sure to fall in again. The rails are on an embankment just opposite our house, which is continually sinking, and they have to relay the track after every wet day—*that* is where *the* accident will occur, which everybody expects someday, and we shall have to take the wounded in. Edward and I have settled all that.

Love to you both and especially to little Carrie

Your affectionate Mother

Catherine A. Hubback

~ 21 ~

My dearest John,

I had your letter enclosing the £100 last week, and while I thank you very much for your kindness and consideration for me I really scruple about your doing so much it seems like robbing your wife and children. I cannot however refuse it now, more particularly as it seems such a great relief to Edward to know that I have something of my own in case I should require anything extra. I have paid $100 of the furniture bill, and Edward says we will pay the rest next month, but having paid so much I do not feel ashamed of seeing Mr Gurnett now. He complained they had been quite lonely without my being there for so long—as to the money, that did not signify! I should hope however next year that we shall not have so much trouble—and that there will be no need of so much help from you. I am sure, so far as my wants are concerned I could *do* as I am, and if my income were £200 a year I should be quite rich. You are only too good to me.

I wish with all my heart that it were possible for Edward to have done with Mr Makin. I know both Mr Blair and Mr Friedlander say so too. But Edward says it cannot be—they must get on as well as they can for another year—and then the partnership ends. He thinks that is only right. I am sure it is not to his advantage in a worldly sense but if it is right, of course it is the thing to do, and he will not be the less respected because he sticks loyally to what is right instead of what seems most profitable. He would be glad enough to do otherwise if he thought it could be so.

We have not heard again from Charlie since he wrote his decision to come here; I hope he is busy making preparations. We shall know where they have settled if they can reach the 10 February steamer. We have this house till May, after that, we shall do as seems best, either about keeping it on, or giving it up—a good deal will depend on what befalls Charlie, and a good deal on what Edward has to do. He wants Mr Makin to stay in England, as he thinks the business goes on better here without him. Everything always happens so differently from what one expects here, and people generally are so constantly changing their plans that *our* uncertainties are only in character with the rest of the Californian world—and I have left off minding them at all. *Alors comme alors.*

I heard lately from both your Aunt Fs—and also picked up a good deal of news from a young German lady, who had been in Hants[53]—so I feel quite posted up in English affairs.

We have had a great storm and quantities more rain; Edward and I had some trouble in getting along our usual Sunday walk—the mud was so deep—but it is not very cold now; everybody declares that they never remember so cold a winter, which I think proves their memory to be very short, as the first winter I was here it froze hard enough to kill all the tender plants, and one other year I saw quite thick ice in Grove Street. The wind and tides yesterday made the bay so rough that people were sick in the ferry boat. I have not been to the City for 3 months I think, but I must go soon as I want some flax thread which I can only get there.

I have nearly got rid of a bad cold and cough which I believe originated in damp boots but it is not well enough to take to Church tonight where Edward is gone without me. I have been taking port wine as a tonic, which I always want after one of these bad colds—in spite of all the denunciations of drinking from temperance people. The President[54] telegraphed all over the country that he did not mean to offer his visitors wine on New Year's day—in which he was wise. If they put a universal stop to 'receiving' on New Year's day it would be an improvement I think. It seemed to me a prodigious waste of time and energy.

I hear that the young ladies' association met a week ago, when an objectionable young man was admitted. I should think that would soon spoil the whole affair. May Kirkham intended to leave it in consequence. They were to meet at each other's houses; but I don't expect they will do much. I might have gone on a little longer as it turns out—but on the whole I am glad to be free of them—and if I have Dina and the children I shall not want them at all at that time.

By the way about the money for Charlie, of course if the interest is not paid annually it will be reckoned due when the principal is. I think I explained all that.

Goodbye.

God bless you

Your affectionate Mother
Catherine A. Hubback

~ 22 ~

My dear Mary,

I have owed you a letter for a long time, but seemed always to have something I was obliged to say to John, so you have not had your due. I had yours of the 31st in which you mention the box you have sent. I have no doubt of liking the dress when it arrives—and I am very much obliged for your continual kindness and thoughtfulness about me. You did not say how the box was to be sent, but I infer it was to come here, as you supposed Charlie and his family were to do. My last letter to John will have explained all that. I should have liked it, I think, but then who knows? and it might not have turned out well, and it would have been my doing. So I have satisfied myself that it is all well—tho' I cannot say I am not disappointed. I did so long for that little boy, and had so many ideas about him. Mr Lywood's offer however seems too fair to refuse, and it saves a great deal of loss their staying.

We will take care to send on the box if it comes here. I shall be very pleased to have a handsome silk gown, and 16 yards will allow of a trained skirt. I never flounce silk—it spoils the effect of the long folds—and I shall wear the California silk which I have now more freely. Black silk is *the* thing here both for old and young in full dress and every occasion.

I hope Harry Smith will be happy, though I do not like cousins marrying—it seems quite clear that he will be poor at all events.

I always want you to tell me about the little girls, I never hear enough of them. I should like to know if Carrie has any notion of her letters yet. Her father used to make capital letters with his bricks and bits of wood, when he was about her age. He used to copy them from shop fronts, and such sort of things. It came to him by nature, as it did to me—I never learnt to read. What does she build with her bricks? Ruins used to be John's great delight—which were easy of construction. Everybody admires her photo and cries out at her dark eyes and light hair as being so pretty.

I am glad you have better accounts of Mrs Boutflower—at her age any illness is likely to be trying to her, and alarming to her friends. Mr H. Holderness is better—he was really very ill with a brain fever which has left him weak. He had a narrow escape for he was found insensible in his room in the evening, and the doctor said he would have been dead if he had remained another half hour without help. It must be a wretched thing to be ill at a great American hotel—but his friends took turns sitting up with him, and he is now at the Cobbs at Alameda.

My pupil Adèle de Fremery has had the mumps and a good deal of fever, her brother James having been laid up with typhoid after mumps—but she is much better now and I expect her to come to me next Tuesday. We have very pleasant times together, as she is very intelligent and well disposed only a little perhaps too old for her age in some things—what some people call 'priggish'—a word I particularly hate: but she has very clever fingers, and I hear is a beautiful musician; her brother amused his convalescent hours, embroidering on Java canvas, a whole set of mats and covers for his mother's toilet, washing table and bureau. I never saw better done work by any woman—it is so accurate and well finished—he is a great schoolboy and has something like a mustache, but he worked away whilst I was sitting there, as if it were the most natural thing in the world.

I was so glad when the Chinese celebration of New Year was over. Jeek came back punctually on Tuesday evening—but it is hard work house cleaning and bedmaking, altho' the worst of all is dishwashing. I don't see how one can help putting one's hands in greasy water, and mine have been rough and uncomfortable ever since. Yes we all agree dishwashing is the worst part of our boys going away—but as the grocer's clerk said—he found many ladies in the kitchen on those two mornings.

This is Washington's birthday today and tomorrow is a national holiday. I wish he had been born in April—it's a much pleasanter time. However we seem to have pretty well done with the rains now, and the sun gets up and sets about 6—for it goes much more slowly here than in England and the days have time to get warm. I have been to Church this evening, the first time since the first Sunday in January—as my cough was not quite gone but I am quite well again now.

Give my love to little Carrie, and the same to you and John.

Believe me

Your affectionate Mother-in-law
Catherine A. Hubback

[NOTE: Letter catalogued as number 23 has been moved to Letter 5.5]

April 26th [1874]

My dear Mary,

I have just filled a glass of flowers, a ring of blue (wild) lupins, and two large white arums in the center. I wish you could see how well they look. Roses are just coming into flower now; my garden is young and backward, and I gathered my first today, a Saffiano, and a Black Prince, but in some gardens the bushes are covered, and I have seen both white and yellow Banksias like cascades, rippling over other trees. One tall oak tree in particular at a corner garden is completely garlanded with white Banksia—I never saw them more beautiful; and the white arums, which are here always called lilies are in every garden. Mine grow close by the garden-tap, and consequently have plenty of water and one plant has 6 or 7 blossoms on it—tho' they are so young.

It is the prettiest time of the year in this country, and the cold seems to have all gone—we have had no frosts to hurt the blossoms, and I hope we shall have a good fruit year. Strawberries are just coming in, as they are late and are of course too dear for reasonable people but with this weather they will soon become plentiful and asparagus which is 25 cents for 5 pounds was never either so cheap or so fine—so large, as broad as two of these lines, and soft almost up to the end.

I made two very pleasant botanising expeditions last week with Adèle de Fremery and her brother; one was to Berkeley on this side of the bay, we drove there in their carriage and came back by the horse cars; and on Friday we went across the bay, and then beyond the city, out to Saucelito, which is a wild and very pretty place, where very few people live; but a great many go over for the day to gather flowers, and eat their luncheons out of doors. I like the de Fremerys very much. Adèle is about 16, and her brother James a little older and there is a younger boy, quite a child who went with us to Saucelito, whose name is Florent. We were a very merry party, and they said they enjoyed it very much. I had wanted very much to go to Sausalito, and for two successive springs had tried to arrange a party to go in vain. And this year we had so many disappointments that I almost began to despair. However we accomplished it at last, very satisfactorily. I *had* been there once before, but Adèle never had, tho' they have lived here all their lives.

I am so glad your brother has such an improved prospect, and more scope for his energies. John told Edward that your mother had reached you safely, and really the journey from Michael to Rock Ferry is so much the worst part that it is a great thing to have accomplished it. Still I think they must have had some regret in leaving a place where they had lived so long, and had so many interests; and I should suppose would miss the garden and the freedom of the country, only I believe you [sic] all of you like a town life much the best.

For my part, I shall be very sorry to leave Oakland when we have to do it. I am like a cat, and hate to change, altho' at the same time, I daresay I should like moving for some things, if I had to do it. However I have quite resolved not to think of going to England this year. Edward does not expect to have to go, but one can never tell how business may turn out. So should he be obliged to go, I should stop short in Virginia, now Charlie has a house—where he will be able to accommodate me, if I can go to him. To cross the Atlantic, unless I could remain 6 months at least would be too much of an undertaking, and as I have always told you, I shall not desert Edward until he marries, if I can help it.

We have killed the first of the chickens I have reared for our dinner today, but I have not been at all successful in hatching chickens. I don't know why, as the hens sit very steadily, but the eggs seem so often to be good for nothing. I don't think I shall try any more, but keep them for laying—and shut them up when they want to sit. I have 6 hens, so I ought to have plenty of eggs. I bring in 3 or so of a day now—as 2 are not laying at all. They are a great amusement to me.

The Kirkhams are going to the Big Trees, and Mrs Blair to New York, and the Elliotts to Santa Cruz, and the Woolseys are gone to a ranch up the country, and Miss MacCann has pupils in the city, and can only come here on Saturdays.

I am very desirous to go to Monterey and see it. A steamer takes one down there in 24 hours or so, for very little, and leaves one for 2 or 3 days—and Edward thinks perhaps next month he may have time to spare; they say Monterey is as beautiful as the bay of Naples—and there is a beach there, with 150 kinds of shells. There are very few shells generally on the Pacific coast—it is too rough. I do hope we shall manage it.

Kiss little Carrie for me, and with love to you both

Believe me

Your affectionate Mother-in-Law
Catherine A. Hubback

~ 25 ~

My dear Mary,

Yes, I should like to see you and your babies very much. I am so glad you have done so well. Do you know I almost envy you having all the pleasure of those little things growing round you? Sometimes I long so for a child again, I feel as if I must adopt one—but then what should I do with it? If I could get one who wanted a mother and had no need of money, how nice it would be.

I have been making you a little thing, a *fauchette*[55] or some such affair, to wear on your head or round you neck when you go out at night, I hope you will like it. I finished it last night, but I think it will have to follow this letter. I made one to send to Bernhardine, which I shall despatch at the same time—hers is blue and white, and yours black and scarlet, which I thought would better suit your complexion.

I heard from my sister at Barfreston last week. She says Janet[56] is staying at Redhill and enjoys it very much.

I am so glad John's choir is so good—the music in St John's where we go of a morning is just dreadful to me, a quartette who keep neither time nor tune—and *will* sing the most flourishing chants.

The congregation of St Paul's have resolved to turn out Mr Turner, their minister—so they have cut down his salary from 200 to 100 dollars a month; and as he has a wife and family increasing he cannot live on that. Is it not a mean shame, after having promised? But such are the ways of this charming country where free Church is the law of the land.

Was it not nice our being able to spend my birthday on Monte Diablo?[57] I think it did Edward so much good, it put business and bothers and Mr Makin and all other nuisances quite out of his head. There were some queer amusing people up there—Americans *are* very amusing very often—and he says he never enjoyed a short excursion more—which I am so glad of because he went to please me.

I must write to John so goodbye

Your affectionate Mother-in-Law
Catherine A. Hubback

My dear John,

I had a note from Mary last week which gave a very good account of her—she will know that I had the thread all right, and am making some yards of lace with it for Mrs de Fremery— also Adèle de Fremery will be glad to take all I can spare, and as I am likely to have another pupil next month who will also want materials, I shall be very glad if you will at the first chance send me some more. If Mary would just get such another little parcel ready, and you had it handy at your office, you might clap it into the hand of the first young man who is coming out here wanting a letter of introduction.

At present I have Adèle—and the two Marsh girls, and I am to have Kitty Kirkham (I daresay she spells her name *Kittie*)— and there is an enthusiastic Mrs Walsh in the City who talked of coming next month—perhaps she may—altogether I expect to clear enough to pay for a trip to Sonoma, where I want to go for a week, or perhaps a fortnight, in September. There is a boarding house there—a very nice place, I am told—and kept by a nice person. It is pretty up there, and the grapes are excellent. It is cheap to reach as one goes by water most part of the way, and boarding is only $10 a week I believe.

We have not any news to enliven you with. There are various opinions as to whether Mr John Wedderspoon means to propose to Miss Alden or not. He ought to mean it, if he does not, for he devotes himself to her, and he is too old to go spooning on merely for amusement like a boy. She is not too young for him either, and would do very well for a stepmother to his two daughters—who would then be able to return to California.

I went over to the City last week—it is quite an event with me to go so far—but I had got my blue merino skirt all dirty first with tar weed and then with red dust, at Monte Diablo, so I had to take it to be cleaned—and I persuaded Edward to meet Miss MacCann and me to see the pictures exhibited at the Art union. It is a treat to see a good European painting now and then. I do not much like Californian ones—tho' they do talk so much about Keith and other artists. The climate of California is not good for pictures. The colours are so bright, and the air so clear that they look hard—or unnatural. The photos are much better than the paintings on that account.

I am glad Francis Austen[58] is going to work at last. I hope his Father and Mother will visit you, but I fancy she goes out very little, and perhaps she may not come. Francis was always a great favorite of mine, he was not very clever, but so thoughtful and good when he was a little boy. I have not seen him however for years—I wonder what he is like. I expect you will find him very pains-taking if not very bright.

I am sorry that St Paul's are going to turn out Mr Turner—we usually go there in the evening, and the chances are we shall not have any body better. He gave offence I believe to some of the leading members—at least to one—Judge Hanley, about some anthems—and they have resolved to freeze him out—by cutting down his salary to $15 a month, and if he will not go then of his own accord to tell him he must. He had $200 a month promised him—of course he had to resign, and leaves in a few weeks.

I heard the other day of some people here, Mr and Mrs Laidlaw, who sent out invitations to 'their silver wedding'—by which means, as all the invited are expected to make presents of silver, they obtained quite a valuable service of plate. I think Mrs Laidlaw the most disagreeable woman I have met here; she is not in California now, or I should have to be very particular before I went to Sonoma to ascertain that she was not there—as she goes there sometimes. She is gone to Paris.

I am so glad your choir flourishes—it would be a treat to hear it. Are Rob and Harry Smith still in it? And has Harry married yet? I forget.

My love to Mary and you, and the children. I sent Mary's *faldette*[59] by post last week.

Your affectionate Mother
Catherine A. Hubback

October 1874–April 1875

Catherine's modest income from lace-making has been eclipsed by the wrongful appropriation of funds by Edward's partner. The setback unfolds in a context of financial unrest—the 'Panic of 1873'—brought on by rampant speculation in railroads and real estate and marked by widespread bank failure.

~ 27 ~

Oakland
October 18th [1874]

My dear John,

Edward tells me there has been a great failure of a French house. I hope you have no concern with them, Schotzman, which will affect many Liverpool houses. There are expected to be failures here, one house they say must crash this week, all owing to the chartering ships and the graingers combinations—and others are very uncertain—yes Edward is well out of it.

The Blairs are gone to New York, and going on to Mexico about his railway. If that succeeds he will I suppose leave the firm, and give all his attention to managing that business instead, which will make his fortune. Like every body else he is disgusted with the wheat trade here.

I have not seen the Makins yet. He is trying to settle up his business with the banks, and the mortgage; as soon as he has raised a new loan (when we shall be paid) he will have to sell off property to pay it—but he can do that probably pretty soon, as the railway makes the land so valuable.

He is very anxious indeed to carry on the partnership, and I am dreadfully afraid Edward will be persuaded into it. Do you think he ought? He says he shall rely greatly on your opinion, and I suppose will state all the circumstances to you. But I do not feel sure of anything Mr Makin says being true. He misrepresents, perhaps unconsciously, influenced by his wishes. I cannot trust him, and he has done Edward so much harm once, why should he have a chance of doing it over again? I do not think he ever cares for anything but his own immediate convenience. He pretends now he had no idea he was distressing us so much by not remitting the money Edward had advanced for him—did not know at all it was mostly mine, and is very sorry, &c &c. All of which to say the least of it must be *lies*. He knew when he went away he took all the money there was, and left Edward without 50 dollars in the bank or office—when he had no right to take more than 300, he took 1000, unknown to Edward to pay some private debts of his own—that was in going to England—then he got Edward to advance money for his taxes and interest—besides having spent over 2000 dollars in the year *more* than his share of receipts—and now he says he did not know, and is very sorry! It provokes me more than all the rest. He reminds me of the dog which used to steal sheep in Scotland, which when hunted by other dogs, always lay down and looked so pitiful that they would not touch him, and then got up and ran away before the man came up—and next day killed more sheep!

I hear Mrs Makin was enjoying herself immensely in England and did not want to come away. Of course, having the reputation of being an heiress, and staying at free quarters at her husband's rich uncle, she could enjoy herself. I think all the worry, vexation, denials, and losses of the failure have come on us—whilst they were gadding about, and having a good time abroad—which considering that the fault was with Mr R. G. Makin seems rather an unfair division. I did not want to see her, but I am inclined now to think that I will because I really think she might as well know the truth a little—and I am quite sure I should very soon let her know that thanks to Mr Makin, our life has by no means been all sunshine and prosperity.

But after all this—I was interrupted and I don't know what I was beginning to say—only I want to know if you think it would be prudent to carry on the business as before. I dread it—and indeed do not believe what Mr Makin said regarding Mr Thorniewell's approving and wishing it. Nothing Edward says will be decided until February so you will have time enough to advise him—and we shall see what Mr Gawne says when he comes down this month.

Edward took me out for a drive yesterday to the Ocean House, and home through the new Golden Gate Park. It was a charming drive. I had never been there before, and we came along 3 miles by the edge of the sea, with great waves rolling in—not much surf for the Pacific, but very green and white. There was not much wind, and it was behind us, and we had a charming black horse, who did not pull, or run away—we drove with quite a slack rein mostly. There were not many other buggies out, to excite him—so I was not frightened, strange horses being always rather suspected objects with me. I had not been out with Edward for a very long time; we had not indulged in such extravagance, but I did enjoy it very much. The Park will be very pretty in 5 or 6 years—the ground is very favorable—varied but not too broken and they have the most charming roads—smooth as a table—it is to be planted quite down to the sands. There is an entrance quite near the Cliff House. Of all horrible places to drive in, I think San Francisco is the worst. The streets are dreadful—holes and stones, and broken wooden pavements, 'bursted up' in one place, sunk down in another, car tracks in every direction, which indeed are the only smooth places to drive on, but which dislocate you when you have to move off. I had never tried it before, and was really surprised to find how much worse it was than I expected. My love to you all.

Goodbye

Your affectionate Mother
Catherine A. Hubback

~ 28 ~

My dear Mary,

I really owe you a letter; and must make this one do as an acknowledgement of the one I had last night from John, which included a photo of the burnt Stage and a draft for £75. Will you tell him? Of course he reads your letters, and I consider that I am writing to you both in one. He is a great deal too good and liberal, and I assure you we have plenty to make us comfortable through the winter. I have had a nice little stove fixed in the chimney in my small sitting room, where I can have a fire lighted in two minutes, which will burn very little, and make the room quite warm: so we shall be having our breakfast in there when it is cold in the morning, and be quite comfortable—our dining room has no chimney, but a place for putting a stove pipe if we wanted one—which we have never done.

I like the photo very much—I look at it and recognize the old look of the houses and church towers. I always wanted one of Liverpool from the river; and though the ferryboats have moved and made their funnels misty they look very natural.

If I can arrange so as to pay you a visit next year I certainly will, but it is impossible to say how things may go—and it would require a good deal of consideration to *leave* Edward comfortably. If he can come too it will be all straight and easy.

We have had a great deal of rain for October when it is usually dry. I suppose the storm was travelling round the world, as it appears you had your share.

Charlie says the frosts have killed his tender plants, and there has been 3 feet of snow on the Nevadas.[60] Today however it is as warm and beautiful as summer and the rain has made all the grass spring so, that the spaces which last Sunday were as brown and bare as a road, are now of a bright green—and my hens have begun to lay again, having finished their moulting.

I was extremely amused by John's account of your children's games—they must have a good deal of imagination to make a *procession* of themselves—and a good memory for what they have seen. If they had been 4 or 5 years older, it would not have been so funny, but I think it shows great talent in little Carrie who is but just 3 I think.

I hope you like Francis Austen. He was always a great favorite of mine, and very steady and well-disposed. Pray tell me what Ernest[61] is like. I used to be afraid he would be hump-backed—I hope that will be outgrown. He was always much the quickest and most mischievous of the boys. I heard from Fanny who is at Torquay that they think you are very kind to Francis and they are very grateful. I should be afraid she would find solitude at Torquay rather dull, in spite of the beautiful scenery, as she has not been used to live alone, and except it may be to a clergyman and his wife she is not very diffusive to strangers or inclined to make new acquaintances.

Mr Makin is very ill with rheumatism. He was not actually in danger when we heard last, but the complaint has spread so much, beginning in his feet, and then going to his back and his head, that it is very serious, as he had had several severe attacks before, and should it go to his heart would probably be fatal. Edward was up there on Tuesday, and took his turn in sitting up and nursing him—Mrs Ross and Mrs Makin were quite worn out. He will I suppose go again tomorrow or next day. It is hard work, as he cannot move himself, and the pain is so great it makes him restless. I must say the young men here are very good to one another. There was always one to sit up with Mr Holderness when he had brain fever, and though Mr Makin is not *very* popular still there are several who have taken turns in nursing him. It is quite a matter of course. If Edward were to be ill, I have no doubt but I should have plenty of help; however, I hope I shall not have to try.

We were obliged to have fires several days last week, but I hope we shall not keep them continuously for some time to come.

We have just been reading the life of Lord Palmerston by Sir H. Bulwer.[62] It is very interesting, and the more so to me because I know something about so many of the people named having lived through so much of the time. I remember him very well, when he came to Portsdown canvassing for the county. Fanny and I were sent out of the room almost immediately, and I always believed it was for fear he should canvas, by kissing us—that being not an unusual way. I felt injured and defrauded—not because I wanted a kiss, which as I was a keen politician and of course a conservative, I should have refused, but because I wanted to hear what was said. I think I was about 14 at the time, but looked much younger.[63] It was more than 40 years ago, but seems scarcely half as much—'Facts are stubborn things,' and it is a fact that I was born in 1818, or else I never should believe I am 56. Suppose I live to be 80 as so many of my family have done, I might live to see your daughters married!! I hope the photos will be successful.

Goodbye

Your affectionate Mother-in-law
Catherine A. Hubback

November 7th 1874
Oakland

My dear John,

California is greatly surprised at finding the wet season set in so much earlier than usual. However the pioneers remember that in '49 it was just the same, beginning in October and being one of the wettest winters ever experienced. That is just my theory. I am sure the weather goes on for about 25 years and then goes back and begins over again.

Our house stands higher than the surrounding streets, altho' the railroad embankment is a good deal above our garden, but the road and foot path are both lower, and as the ground falls away completely at the corner of 7th and Filbert, the floods run down there in rivers, which our neighbours have to cross, but we have not.

Everything is green, the enclosures and the streets, and the hills; grass grows faster than one can imagine, and we have a bright soft day after a wet one, which makes everything look lovely. Mr Makin is getting better, but I suppose this damp weather will keep him back. It makes me rather rheumatic when it rains and blows all day. Then I get Edward to rub my shoulder with some strong imbrocation which smells of ammonia and oil of thyme—and which has done me a great deal of good.

Last Monday I went to Morse to be Photod—and had two views taken of which I will send you copies. I daresay they will be good when they are done, as they soften and smooth them and make them very flattering. They will not be in time for a real birthday present—somehow I forgot that the 24th was so

29.

My dear John,

California is greatly surprised at finding the wet season set in so much earlier than usual. However the pioneers remember that in '49 it was just the same, beginning in Oct br & being one of the wettest winters ever experienced. That is just my theory. I am sure the weather goes on for about 25 years & then goes back & begins over again. Our house stands higher than the surrounding streets, altho the rail road embankment is a good deal above our garden, but the road & foot path are both lower, and so the ground falls away completely at the corner of 7th & Filbert. the floods run down there in rivers, which our neighbours have to cross but we have not. Everything is green, the enclosures & the streets, & the hills; grass grows faster than one can imagine, and we have a bright soft day after a wet one, which makes every thing look lovely. Mr Makin is getting better, but I suppose this damp weather

9 First page of Letter 29. (*MS. Eng. lett. e. 150, fol. 75*)

10 Envelope from Letter 29 (*MS. Eng. lett. e. 150, fol. 77*)

near until last week—and did not get them done in time. They *say* they take a week doing them.

I was glad to hear of Paul [failed to decipher] again, Charlie had often wondered what had become of him. Tell him to employ a leisure half hour in writing to Charlie—who will be glad to hear of him.

So Birkenhead has at last its Member—which of his sons means to stand? They are none of them his equals, and if they fill his seat [they] will never really take his place. It will be a great loss no doubt, but when people have plenty of money they are sure to find consolation—it is only *poor* people who really suffer in this world.

It was very good of you to give Francis and Ernest the pleasure of meeting. Of course Ernest is well mannered and more *au fait* than Francis, not only having been at sea, which gives boys aplomb of itself, but he was always made so much of by his grandmother from a baby—he *never* could do wrong and was never snubbed or found fault with—and he used to be a great deal with her. Mrs Tragett's manners would have been perfect if they had not been a little artificial—a soupçon of insincerity which flavoured them unpleasantly.

I enclose two little pictures, one for each little girl—I don't know whether they are meant for robins—or some American bird. The Pheasant may be freely translated the *talking* Pheasant, as Edward suggests. Also some lines which I cut out of Harper and which Mary can read to the little ones. I think they are very charming—and feel sure they are English, or else they would [say] robin or bobolink, oriole, thrush or linnet. Perhaps you may have had them before. I hope Carrie has a book to paste all the pictures in that I send her.

I have been making myself a black velveteen mantle, to be trimmed with grebe.[64] I could not get anything in the shape of a round cloak here—at the cloak store the lady so gravely informed me that '*ladies* never wore such things now,' that I almost felt as if I had been asking for a jacket and knicker-bockers at best. However I found a pattern in November Harper—and have nearly finished it. It is too hot yet to wear fur or velvet—but I suppose I shall want it by and bye.

I have just had 2 pair of my English winter boots resoled, and triumphantly told the maker that I had worn one 5 and one 4 winters. 'Such very superior leather' he was obliged to own with a sigh, and English boots I told him are channel soled—not sewed at the side—and so they don't turn up at the edges. He was obliged to own it was too true. American leather is just like American public morality—got up in a hurry to look fine and attract, but no durability or solid strength in it. They laugh at the English because the *Court Circular* is published and read—but after all it is much less coarse and low to care how the queen is than to publish details of Mrs Frank Grant's gowns, or the finery of 'Nellie'—Princess Alice[65] it is said, has written a novel. I wonder whether she still views the world as she did when she cried out, 'Look at those little princesses washing their feet.' I don't see indeed what she can know of life except Princesses. Who would ever tell her the truth about the rest of mankind?

Goodbye. Love to you all.

Your affectionate Mother
Catherine A. Hubback

30

November 29th [1874]
Oakland

My dear Mary,

You will I suppose be home again before this time. I hope you had a very pleasant visit, and left your family well. What a change it must be going to the populous Leicester after the comparative desert of Michael, where your visits used to be paid.

Mr Joseph Hubback arrived here on Friday night, and Edward saw him for a few minutes yesterday. He is to see him again tomorrow in a less hurried way perhaps—though unless things are greatly changed everybody who does see Mr Hubback has to be in a hurry. At least it used to be so formerly—one always had to wait an hour or two and then found he could only spare 3 minutes.[66]

If they could have chosen their weather they could hardly have selected 3 lovelier days than the Friday when he was crossing the state and the 2 days he has been here—no weather in England can compare with such days as come here in the rainy season. The air is as transparent and pure as Lake Tahoe, the dust is all gone; everything is washed, and the grass is as green as England—whilst the tints are only to be described by some lines which always come to my mind describing an Eastern States spring—'The hills are heavenly, blue and brightly tender, And now the sun is as a giant strong.' There are so few deciduous trees here that they make hardly any difference when they do shed their leaves—the Australian wattle trees, of many kinds are just coming into blossom and they are beautiful as John knows. Narcissus are coming into bloom, and I suppose my colored primroses will soon put out buds. Arums always flourish now, and carnations and fuchsias never leave off blooming, whilst mignonette keeps on coming up fresh, and I have sweet peas almost in bloom.

I reckon you will get the photos next week, I hope you will like them. There is one for your book, and the mounted one you can frame and hang in the nursery and overlook the children. They have a way of flattering one very much in those special photos—but they only took a week to finish them after I decided which I would have—and I had them home in less than a fortnight from the day I sat. I expect you will get them therefore before I have your new ones.

I suppose Miss Croft will be arriving at the City next week—John has not sent us word however what steamer she was to go on by—perhaps he did not know.

I have not heard from Charlie for a fortnight. I daresay it has been very cold with them, as it has been so wet here—5 inches of rain in one storm of 36 hours—in November—is pretty heavy—a forewarning of what is to come. Was there fog on John's birthday? There was one the day he was born 30 years ago—and such a cold winter afterwards.

The young women here have buttoned themselves up so tight *à l'antique*, from the waist to the feet that they can hardly sit down—and I expect the next thing will be to slit their dresses down the side as Venus and those antiques used to do. I suppose in that case they would wear underclothing however—which at present many of them don't seem to have.

I am going to put some seeds in this letter; for Carrie you shall sow them in a pot and call them Grandmama's flowers.

Love to you all

Your affectionate Mother-in-law
Catherine A. Hubback

31

April 4th [1875]

My dear John,

I have just received your letter of the 11th, and as I did not write by Monday's mail, I shall answer it at once. We decided that the way by the Isthmus, tho' longer, would be much easier for me alone than the cars, as this time of year the latter are not at all to be depended on for the snows are not all gone tho' many of the bridges are, and I have not seen the other route, and want to see it, and may have no other chance. I must of course come back by the plains; but before the snow falls the route will be good enough. You don't know what it is to live day and night for 8 days in one of those cars, with all sorts of people, and surrounded by what one may call all the indecencies of civilised life. I often hear people say they enjoy it, but it is quite incomprehensible to me. I am going tomorrow to take my berth in the *Montana* to start the 19th, and Edward will write to Mr [failed to decipher] to take a passage in the *Algeria* for the 15th—she's a beautiful boat. and perhaps will be less crowded than those which don't carry Steerage passengers. Of course I must take my chance of my companions.

I don't want to spend a night in New York in going. I shall go to the Brevoort hotel and leave my great box in charge, and then on by the night mail to Virginia. I shall reach Gainesville, if all goes well next morning. Of course, the *when* depends upon what passage we make. I shall be glad if Mr [failed to decipher] can meet me, I rather depend on him, but I am to be under the care of the Captain on both sides of the continent, and mean to sit at his table. Everybody here says I shall enjoy the trip very much, and that tho' longer, it is much less disagreeable than the cars. I have plenty of money for my passage even tho' they have raised the steamer fares 35 dollars.

The reason I did not write by Monday's mail was that we were going to start that day for the Geysers, and I wanted to tell you if we came home safe—which we have done. I enjoyed it extremely, tho' I am very tired today. We went up on Monday by boat and rail to Cloverdale where we slept, next morning taking a stage for the Geysers. The drive lasted from 7:30 to 12, and was very magnificent tho' a little 'skary'—now and then we had only about 3 inches of road to spare, but I was not at the edge and did not see so much. We were to sleep at the Geyser hotel, so we were not hurried and had plenty of time to look about.

The cañon is very grand, the geysers themselves rather a humbug in my opinion. I had expected something bigger and more terrible. It's queer to see all that fussing and bubbling and steaming. I daresay some day it will all blow up again, there must be a good deal of firing up going on down there to work all the engines—but I did not seem to expect it was going to blow up then. I daresay if I had gone in thin boots I might have spoilt them, but I had an old pair of English ones, and really they were none the worse. Yesterday we started at 8 and drove till 2, then rail from Calistoga and Vallejo, and home by boats, reaching this house at ten—a good day's work—especially after 2 bad beds. At Cloverdale neither of us slept a wink—and at the Geysers I was not much better.

That drive out of the Cañon over a mountain 3700 feet high which we got up in a waggon and 4 horses was never to be forgotten. I was on the outside, it being better that the weight should be inward, and I declare my companion, an elderly man, was more frightened than I was. Edward and

11 A mudwagon of the type described by Catherine (Letter 31) carries visitors to the Geysers. A well-preserved example is on display at the Oakland Museum of California. The image, *c.* 1880, is taken from a stereo card by photographer Andrew Price. (*Library of Congress, Washington, DC*)

Miss MacCann were on the driver's seat—and there were 5 others in the waggon, except when they walked uphill. I assure you I set my teeth and held my breath many times. If I had stretched out my arm I could have dropped a stone straight down into the river at the bottom, between one and two thousand feet below us. We had good horses and a capital driver, and the road was mostly 5 or 6 inches wider than the wheels, but in some spots, where it had been washed out by late rains, and just mended, one did not feel sure it would not sink again, and it made one feel creepy.

We had Foss from Pine Tree flat to Calistoga. He upset last year and killed a lady, and since he has been more cautious. He drives very well, but not better than the others, and the road was much less frightful, and he had 6 horses, so we got along in fine stile. There were *men* who said they would not take the same drive again for 100 dollars. I don't want to take the same I admit, but I hope to take others like it. I should like to go to the valley and to see the Big Trees.

I hope you are not going to worry me about remaining in England. It will be hard when I come so far to see you if you spoil my visit. This must be my home until Edward has a wife, and if I had to stay in Europe for a winter I should have to find a warmer climate than England. Anyhow unless prevented by any misfortune, I mean to return here before winter, and I want to spend October in Virginia first. I shall be very busy next week, as I have to pack away everything for storing.

Love to you both, and the little ones.

Your affectionate Mother
Catherine A. Hubback

December 1875–December 1876

Catherine has returned from her journey, having seen John and Charles for the first time in more than four years and made acquaintance with their growing families. In her absence, Edward has found work as an agent for the Stockton Transportation Company at 109 California Street, San Francisco. They resume householding at 1128 Myrtle Street.

~ 32 ~

December 19th
1875

My dear John,

I was very glad of your joint letter last Friday; it had seemed a long time since I had heard from you, altho' I suppose it was only because I had been doing so much settling in our house and getting everything straight. I am much better and stronger tho' my back is still stiff and sometimes painful, and I cannot walk far or fast, nor can I bear the motion of a carriage, so that I sometimes wish I could go about in a palanquin or hammock— and I have not yet ventured to Church, as I am afraid of the stiff straight backs. I hope to do so on Christmas day at least.

I like the house very much, now we have fitted in. We were rather too big at first—had too many chairs and tables, but we do very well now, and having fewer rooms makes so much less to look over and find fault about.

I am happy to say that Edward's Company is going on now very prosperously; it took a little while to start, and there is always a good deal to learn in a new business; but he says they know now how to do things well and economically, and just what everything costs, and he expects if next year brings a good harvest it will pay all its own past expenses. They have been bringing down sheep from the San Joaquin valley, which pays very well, and the farmers are very much pleased with the conveyance and have a good many hundreds or thousands perhaps more to send.

Altogether Edward is recovering his spirits, and having a home again is a great thing. Miss Bentley assured me he used to moan sadly over my absence. One likes to be missed a little. I have seen very little of Miss Bentley, the girl he likes so much—as we only called there last afternoon, and it was too dark to see much then. Only I saw she was not tall, and heard that she had an American accent, which I never can like, and her name is Florence. She is young, and I don't think Edward is badly in love with her altho' he certainly likes her very much.

I have not seen many people here. Mrs Blair comes whenever she can, but I cannot walk so far as her house yet. We have very nice houses round us, no bad shanties, as there were down on 6th and 7th but I do not know most of the people even by name. Our next neighbour called on me, and seemed a pleasant person, but as she keeps no servants, she must be always busy, and I cannot imagine that she can have much time for visiting. She must be what Yankees term a *capable* woman and get along without any help; but they are only 2 and have not been long married.

Did you know that Clayton—the firm Mr Makin joined, failed just afterwards and lost a great deal? He is now doing nothing, and has had rheumatism again. They had made too large advances to farmers, upcountry, and the harvest being so short, they were not repaid.

I hear from my sister that Helen Purvis has married again, a man about as poor as herself—what fools some people are! Experience does not even make them wiser.

I find my fur cloak very delightful to walk about in, during this cold spell. We have had pretty sharp frosts at night, but it seems likely to change now. Ever since we have been here we have had sunshiny days and blue skies.

I am glad the Government were awake in time to take Egypt in hand.[67] I wonder whether Mr Scudamore will ever be paid or will it be in Turkish bonds?

Love to you all.

Believe me

Your affectionate Mother
Catherine A. Hubback

33

December 26th
Oakland

My dear Mary,

I am sorry to learn from John's letter to Edward that you have been out of health. Charlie makes the same complaint of Dina—perhaps *circumstances* have something to do with it, and that you will be better by the time this letter reaches you.

I have been regularly gaining strength since I came here, and am much better now, more active and able both to walk and sit better than I was any time in England. My back is still stiff—I want a hinge somewhere below the waist, or the bones want oiling. Sometimes I can lace my boots, sometimes not, then my China boy does it—but I have no pain now except when I try to do too much for me—or when I move after sitting still a good while. I went to Church yesterday for the first time—and bore it very well considering. It is 10 blocks to walk to reach it. It was a lovely day, and we had no fire in the drawing room. Today has been pouring with rain, and the damp obliges one to have a little blaze tho' it is not cold.

I told Edward about your children being threatened with a summons and he was extremely amused. However he thought it a pity that when the policeman came to apologise you did not give him half a crown, and tell him not to be such a goose again. He would then have been your admirer and devoted servant for life. That is Edward's way. He never quarrels with anyone, and makes friends somehow instead.

I wish Arthur Higginton had come to see him when he passed thro' San Francisco—then he would have learnt the facts about that box which never turned up, and about which Edward took such trouble, whereas he went his way under the impression as he told Mr Holderness that Edward had behaved very ill to his family.

The Transportation Company have been doing a good deal more business this month, and as their means become better known they will no doubt have some more employers. Three times last week, I called Edward at half past five that he might be in the City by 7—and twice he breakfasted at 7:15. When he goes out so early he breakfasts in the boat—but I do not sleep much after waking to talk to him.

Having my old servant Kew, I have had no trouble about returning to housekeeping, and we have a very nice little boy under him, who mostly waits on me, and is in fact housemaid. Kew has done a great deal of gardening in consequence in the back yard, which is larger than yours, and open to the sun and air. We have put in one crop of peas, and next week I shall make him put in some more, and get some good rhubarb plants, which I mean to cover and blanche—a thing they never do here, so the rhubarb is very green and late. Gooseberries do not thrive here, and apples are not very good, altho' so beautiful to look at, so rhubarb is of more value as a substitute. I did not make any mince meat, it seems hardly worth while for only two, but I gave Edward a capital Christmas pudding, which I made myself for fear of mistakes.

I am reading Baron DeHübner's wanderings round the world—which interests me extremely, tho' here and there he is certainly inaccurate, as when he speaks of its freezing in June at San Francisco. It is only cold by comparison.[68]

I have called on the Bentleys and seen the girl Edward likes so much.

I am going to change my machine for a Willcox & Gibbs—
Wanzers don't exist here—and I want it for my embroidery—a
hand one, of course. It runs very light and makes no noise.[69]
I must leave off.

Believe me yours affectionately
Catherine A. Hubback

34

January 2nd 1876

My dear John,

At last we have received the box. It had been some days at the Custom House, and then went to the appraiser's store—where they said they waited for the key! However as the key never came they seem to have done without—I am sure they never opened it at all. Nothing was moved, and everything came quite right. Edward is delighted with the cruet stand which just suits the small table. I hope to teach the boys to use the dusters and cloths—they seem at present to prefer keeping them in a box. The pillow cases are quite large enough, I was afraid they were too small when I first saw them.

By the way have you seen any of the paper blankets which I saw by the papers were patented in England? Brown paper, four or five pence apiece, and as warm as a woolen one. They must be rather *crackly* I should think, and would not *tuck* in well. In fact I do not much believe in them. But if brown paper is so very warm it would be rather good for lining the bodies[70] of dresses instead of wadding. I think I shall try it, for that purpose next time I make a winter jacket.

The rain has come back again. It has rained a little most evenings since Christmas, and tonight it is pouring, and it has come on so gradually that I suppose we shall have another wet spell. We have had very few cold mornings, and several days last week I never lighted a fire at all. When the sun shines this room is very warm of an afternoon. I suppose it will be hot in summer—but I like sunshine and warmth.

I wanted to go to Church yesterday but the rain did not stop until too late—but I did go today, and was able to remain for the whole Service, which is the first time for many months—indeed since I left California—and after all I was not nearly so much tired as I was in England anytime—and I walked both ways, so you may understand how much I am improving.

Mrs Kirkham has sent to ask us both to her house Friday evening. I said I was afraid to go out at night, but Mrs Blair declared she would take no excuses if it was a fine night—luckily it rained hard, and even Edward preferred to stay at home—in consequence Miss May gave herself great airs on Saturday when Edward called there, and took on herself to be much affronted; whereas Edward in reality was engaged if he went out at all to go somewhere else so her indignation was quite uncalled for.

They had a most successful Sunday school tree on Monday, the first time such an affair has been well arranged. Unfortunately the very able superintendent is going to give it up—and the school which had got into nice order will be sure to go back if it falls into Mr Akerly's hands—as with the best intentions in the world he is no better than a child.

The Herds have not sent home my sewing machine yet—and as they seemed so reluctant to part with it, I have offered that they should keep it at half price. I saw a nice little Wilcox & Gibbs for $26—to which a hand winch could be put, but of course I must have money to pay for it and I do not want to *trust* the Herds—having a lively remembrance of what you told me. As they have had it now 9 months free of charge, and it would have cost them $2 a month to hire one, they ought to think themselves very well off, and not keep me waiting for it. I daresay they have not got the money, but then I have not got the machine.

I shall hope to have a good account of Mary when you write, and that before you read this that she will be doing well and through her troubles. I hope the children came back all safe. Did they go to the Zoo Gardens and see a real elephant?

Love to them all

Your affectionate Mother
Catherine A. Hubback

~ 35 ~

May 21st [1876]
Oakland

My dear John,

I had your two letters last Saturday—yesterday—Edward brought them when he came back after being up at Sacramento. He left me on Tuesday, and did not get back till yesterday, being kept waiting there for their boats, which were delayed by the strong current in the river. The water is very high and in one place has broken through the levée flooding a great deal of the country back of the river. Then he came back in their own tug, and there was a furious storm on Friday night which obliged them to lie to and wait till morning. He went up in the passenger boat, and she was so crowded there was not even room for him to sit down, but like Tom in the book[71] which I told you about, 'he had to stand up all night'—walking about on deck to keep himself warm.

I did really go to the pic-nic on the 13th and liked it. It was a bad day—cold and windy, and the dust was blinding—but we had a pleasant party—and I have been none the worse since for my ten hours' exertions. So you see how strong I am—indeed I can walk very much better than I can sit still. I walked about 3 miles last Tuesday well enough to pay some visits. I get very stiff sitting still, like a sewing machine which wants oiling—but I don't need to lie down, and am not to any outward appearance crippled. Everybody says how well I am looking, and the dresses I had made in England want letting out—and if ever I can get my guard ring off my finger, I will have it stretched a little—it is thick enough to bear that.

I forget whether I told you I had been getting up a new society for missions[72] that is to work for missions. I hope we shall raise something for that—they want it badly. The society has only just been started, and is not arranged exactly like the former one. At present I have only 7 members—young ladies here all protest they are so overwhelmed with occupation One part of our plan is to have a reunion on the last Saturday evening in each month, first to see what has been done, and then make ourselves agreeable for a couple of hours. To this gentlemen are to be admitted, and perhaps we may make it pleasant. It is to be held at different houses, so the entertainment may be varied—but it is a settled point that there is to be no expense in the way of ices or oysters.

I suppose Mary is going to Llangollen, with the children but you neither of you say so. I have been through the valley once and remember it very well. There was an 'observation car' attached to the railroad in which I travelled, and we could see the prospect very well—especially as there was only one other person in the car so I could move about and look out.

I do not know what the persecution of the Chinese will end in. They have passed a decree to shave all their heads if committed to prison, and they are constantly committing them for all sorts of things which they don't notice in any other people. Then they lay heavy taxes on their laundries—they tried it two years ago, and the Chinese beat them in a suit at law.[73] Now they say they can't afford to go to law again, but shall wait till the proper representations are made by the Chinese authorities—they being quite aware that the tax is an infringement of their rights secured by treaties. Of course there is danger that the injustice here will be retaliated on Americans in China—and I suppose the other states would not like to give up the Chinese trade, however, the Californians may resolve to drive them out of the country.

They are going to have grand doings at the commem-
oration[74]—the 1st and 2nd services in all the Churches with
appropriate sermons. I shall certainly *not* go on Saturday—and
on Sunday I shall try to get to Alameda where the clergyman
is English. I can't really stand an *appropriate* sermon—then one
day there is to be a salute fired with 'shotted guns' from all the
forts in the Bay—and fireworks and illuminations at night. I
expect they will blow somebody's head off, or sink some ship
with their shotted guns. If the inhabitants had all lived in the
neighbourhood of Portsmouth they would know better than
to allow such things. And as under ordinary circumstances the
4th is always celebrated by 2 or 3 houses being burnt, what
will be the chances on this occasion? Do you remember the
regiment of Irish dragoons—no volunteers, who wanted to
pillage Bradford—to put loaded cartridges in their rifles at a
review, and then did set fire to the barracks at Portsmouth and
plunder the officers' quarters? My fear is that the Irish here
may do something of the sort against the Chinese. It would be
a fine chance during the processions and tom-fooleries on the
4th, when all the fire brigade will be out in the procession, and
of course out of the way of a fire in the Chinese quarter. A fire
when everything is dry and the wind blowing as it always does
in July, would be something serious.

They have been trying to collect a centennial fund in
Oakland, and succeeded in raising $78—which testified to
the general good sense of our fellow townsmen. Some boys
in San Francisco were detected as the agents of burglaries,
which they confessed had been undertaken to raise funds to
go to the Centennial—they had made $22 by their industry.
There have been a great many burglaries about Oakland too. I
don't know whether they originated in an equally praiseworthy
desire for enlargement of ideas, and acquisition of knowledge.

That is one reason why people think me so brave because I don't mind being left with only little Phun in the house. How should anybody know? Phun could only tell his countrymen, and I am not afraid of them. I never hurt any of them—and I don't believe they would hurt me.

Goodbye. I suppose Mary will be at Llangollen when you get this.

Your affectionate Mother
Catherine A. Hubback

36

May 28th [1876]
Oakland

My dear John,

I suppose your family will be in Wales when you get this letter, tho' I am not clear whether Mary is going or not.

I suppose I shall be alone again next week for some days, as Edward will be going up the river for the first or second cargo of wheat, and that they expect will be about the 10th or so. There is such an enormous crop, and so few boats to carry it, that there will be pretty hard work to get it down. I do hope Edward will have a 'good time' at last. What is to be done with all the grain when it is here, I can't imagine, unless you have a famine in Europe and want it all. But that does not concern me much, so long as the Company get plenty of work. There will not only be the commission for Edward's share of work, which we hope will be about $300 a month, but there will be the dividend in November—so I trust there will be something realised to pay debts.

The block in which Edward's office is was burnt last week—that is the top and back behind the offices, where there were 3 large stories. The offices were not burnt but drowned by the water poured in from above—Edward's amongst others—he had not much to spoil—but things were not dry yesterday—and it must be all cleared out. His papers and books were all soaked. It will not be *that* part of the city which will be burnt on the 4th I expect—Dupont and Jackson Streets and thereabouts are the Chinese quarters.

I had a reunion last night. I think I told you I had got together a missionary society again—we have not many members, and have not all managed to meet yet—but we agreed we would have a social meeting once a month at each other's houses—I had the first as President last night. There were only 3 girls present—the others were away or busy—but we had 4 gentlemen—Mr Hassell who was extremely merry and pleasant, and the brothers of two of the girls, one pretty well, the other a decided prig—however we had a very lively evening. I wanted Miss MacCann and her brother who would have helped us on, but they had an engagement she could not escape. I expect the Vice President will have the next—their house is larger and they have a piano and can dance. We might have managed ten in our room, and I could have found chairs for them—not more very well. We had out the letters,[75] at which Mr Hassell is very expert and Jozey Lemon found out 'bayonet' in ten minutes—tho' her brother had always to be helped to the first and last letter, and Mr Smith kept on saying in a condescending way—'*I* don't know much about this sort of thing'—as if anybody cared. Florence Bentley, who is a favourite of ours was away unluckily—I have a Miss Beleher, Miss Bentley and Miss Benton. It was very encouraging last night.

I like the name for Charlie's boy very much—they say he is very thriving—Dina must have her hands full with the 3 children and house. Charlie sent me the plan of the new house, which they are preparing to build. It will have 4 rooms and an outside kitchen. I hope it will be weather-tight which their present abode is not.

Mr Johnson turned up here last week, and Edward saw him. He will be going to England soon he says. He has been travelling all this time.

Goodbye

Your affectionate Mother
Catherine A. Hubback

37

Oakland
July 30th [1876]

My dear Mary,

I had a letter from you last week, and I am looking forward to having the kettle-holder which Carrie promises me with great pleasure. Pray tell her it is the very thing I want, though not exactly for a kettle, but for the blower which often gets very hot, when one leaves it on a while. I shall keep the holder for that in the drawing room, where is the only grate we have; our dining room having a stove, and the bed-rooms none at all. I assure you I shall be very proud of my granddaughter's performance, and when I show it, people will say, 'oh yes, she is English, so no wonder.' American girls of five years old, learn to dance and to dress, and often wear rings and ear-rings, but don't often learn anything else—I know of one of 12 who has no idea of using a needle. I hope Carrie had my letter in good time; I did not forget her birthday yesterday.

I have not yet been able to decide anything about going away for change, I do not much fancy going to the great and fashionable baths. I have however written to our landlord's wife to ask if she will take me as boarder for a week or two at Coloma. It is a lovely country, and in the middle of orchards— amongst the foot hills of the Nevada, and on one branch of the American river. I should prefer boarding in a private family to a hotel, and Mrs Weller's mother having invited me, gives me a reason for offering. It is the American way to 'offer to board' and gives no offense as it might elsewhere. I want very much to see that part of the country, and I expect the air would be more bracing than Oakland at this time of year.

It has been unusually hot at times all this summer, and I find it very relaxing. It is so very seldom we have anything like heat here. The papers predict an early wet season; and unless we have a thunder-storm or two, which is not usual, we may expect the alternative of earthquakes to work off superfluous electricity. People here however generally have decided that there is no more danger of 'shakes'– and all through Oakland are building tall 3 story houses, which would be very unpleasant residences should there be a repetition of the earthquakes of former times.

Edward's work goes on; the rivers have not yet fallen too low for the boat, but the prices are so low for wheat they are storing a great deal at Stockton to wait. This is in *our* warehouse mostly, so the Company will have a double advantage, as of course it will have to come down by it someday.

I heard a puzzle last night which you must ask—as of course you will see it when written. What does *bac–Kac–he* spell? It sounds very queer.

Love to John and the little ones

Your affectionate Mother-in-law
Catherine A. Hubback

38

Oakland
August 6th [1876]

My dear John,

I have a letter from you and one from Mary to acknowledge—the latter with the kettle-holder from dear little
Carrie. I admire it very much and shall find it very useful in
the winter when we have fires again. I shall be proud to show
it to my friends as the work of a little maiden of 5 years old.
Miss MacCann thought it quite wonderful—and I shall hold it
up as an example to Californian girls of twelve years old.

I am very sorry to find from your letter that you are so
troubled about your business. To lose hope and spirit is the
worst loss you could have except perhaps health, in the way of
business. It is quite natural that you should be anxious, but you
ought not to give way to despondency, since your difficulties
do not come from any fault of your own, and so long as you
continue to do what you believe to be right, you may feel
sure you will be helped through all the perplexities which are
troubling you. It is exactly in such cases that may be applied
the command to take no thought for the morrow, for sufficient
unto the day is the evil thereof. We have no right to expect that
we shall never have any trouble, but quite the contrary, only we
have to trust that the trouble will not be greater than we can
bear if we take it in the right way. That is to do our duty as well
as we can, and bear patiently until comfort or relief come, and
not take any rash or unwise steps to conquer or avoid trouble
in a hurry. As our Saviour you remember waited when he was

hungry, until relief was sent, instead of turning the stones into bread as he was tempted to do.

I think you were quite right to take your holiday in Wales as you did, and I know from experience that it is not laying out a definite sum in such a way that can be considered extravagant; you go, spend so much, and come back and there's an end of it. It is worth the money. Economy and extravagance are not affairs of a day or a week, but the result of everyday actions, in watching over all the small items of daily life, or the reverse.

I hear and read everywhere of the bad times, notwithstanding the low prices of everything, nobody seems the richer. When sewing machines were invented it was expected that the needle-work of a family would be so easily got through that there would be time for all the elegancies of life. But the result has been that the extravagance of dress has increased with the facility of making it, and whereas a gown formerly could be easily made in two or three days, it now takes 2 people hard work for a week to make a suit, and about twice as much material. It is the same in everything else; at least in America: if things are cheap, people will not buy them. The only people who seem to be rich here are those who cheat or steal in some way. Of course they don't call it by such names, but that is the truth.

Edward was very busy all last week, he only dined at home once between last Sunday and today, and he was out two nights at Vallejo where most of his work was last week—out at 6 and not back till ten or eleven the next day.

Nearly all the children in our street have the whooping cough: there are a great many of them.

I have not yet decided anything about going away yet, perhaps I may not go away at all. I think it is drier and dustier this year than ever. They say we shall have early rains. I don't know why.

The San Joaquin river is falling rapidly, and Edward expects they will soon have to draw off the boats. Then the grain the farmers have been keeping back will be left there till the rains as there is no way to move it out the river.

My love to the [failed to decipher]

Your affectionate Mother
Catherine A. Hubback

39

Oakland
August 28th [1876]

My dear Mary,

I have two letters of yours to acknowledge at once; as during Edward's absence I did not have any. He was over a week up at Colusa and Princetown and came back looking very brown and baked. It does him a great deal of good having to run about the country so much and his expenses being paid makes it all the more agreeable. He says there is wheat enough up the river there to employ them to the end of the year and bring down so there is no fear of there not being work for their barges.

I am very much grieved at your troubles and anxieties. It is a great comfort to me to think that *you* are of a cheerful, trustful disposition. John is always inclined to be too anxious and doubtful. Perhaps the present trouble is to teach him to be more trustful. More conscientious and desirous to do what is right I know he cannot be, but like everybody in this life he must have his good and bad times, to try and perfect his character. For nearly 30 years now I have had so much of change and disappointment and uncertainty in everything, mixed up with so much of good and so many helps and blessings, that I always feel when things are going well or ill that it will probably not last, and I feel quite sure that you will be helped through now. But of course I know that trouble *is* trouble whilst it lasts, and however hopefully and cheerfully borne, it does not cease to be a trial. Still whilst both you and the children have health you have one of the greatest blessings.

I have not heard from Charlie for 3 weeks, and am getting very anxious about him, as Dina had been very ill, with intermittent fever when he wrote last, and tho' better he said she was terribly reduced.

I am delighted with little Carrie's letter and am very glad mine reached her on the right day.

What would you think of Californian ideas when I tell you, there is a debt on our Church of 500 dollars for grading the street opposite, and it was suggested to raise this money, that the young people of the congregation should represent a series of tableaux from the *Pilgrim's Progress*, such as Christian dropping his burden at the Cross and the angels clothing him, Christian fighting with Apollyon, and various others, culminating in Christian being received by angels at the gates of the Celestial city? People rather objected it would be expensive or difficult, but thought it would perhaps do a great deal of good! If our Church did not adopt it, there was some other congregation who would. When I was asked, I could not avoid saying I thought it would be rather profane, and that if they wanted to represent something new let them take one of Scott's novels or something secular, and leave out both angels and devils, considering the quality of a mixed Californian audience. What they will do I don't know—the money has to be paid, it being one of the peculiarities of this country, that streets are graded or macadamised quite irrespective of the wishes of the dwellers on them, but the owners of the property have to pay the cost. In this case the Episcopal Church has one side of the block, and the Roman Catholic the other. I expect they will eventually have a concert, and dance and raise the money.

With love to you all

Believe me

Your affectionate Mother-in-law
Catherine A. Hubback

~ 40 ~

My dear Mary,

I had your letter from Leicester on Friday evening when Edward came home. He had been away from Monday morning at 6 o'clock when I sent him off with a cup of coffee and a slice of melon, and only returned on Friday about 6 in the evening. He was very successful however in the business about which he was sent, and gave great satisfaction to his employers.

I hope you contrived to enjoy your visit to Leicester, in spite of the *contretemps* about Sarah. I wish you could send a more satisfactory account of your Mother, but it must be a great satisfaction to you all that she is not in the Isle of Man, but where her children are all within a tolerably easy distance of her. She could hardly be in a more central place than Leicester. How she must have enjoyed having our grand children with her.

I am glad Caroline has finished the great Work satisfactorily, and I have no doubt of its beauty. Pray how did Mrs Segar get through hers, and was the whole completed?[76]

Certainly I am very different from what I was at this time last year, when I could not move any way without pain. I have got rid of the stiffness now which used for a long time to come on when I sat still, and made getting up such an effort. My back is sometimes a little weak still, but there is nothing perceptible in my movement for our opposite neighbour always declares I go about like a young girl. *She* is a grandmother too, and very active and energetic. I am plumper also than ever I was, so much so that the bodies made in England are too tight for me to be quite comfortable—and *I* don't wear any padding or springs under them.

One would be surprised to see the finely developed busts and regular figures of all the women here, so nearly of a size and shape, if one were not let into that piece of natural history that they owe their figures to the dressmaker just as much as their costumes—whilst as to teeth and hair, as a matter of course they are supplied as needed; and I have been assured that there is scarcely a toilet table in the country where the Chinese rouge is not kept ready for use, as that is considered the only kind not hurtful. I remember once seeing a little book of it, which my father had brought from China so long ago, and it was green and coppery until you wetted it, and I have no doubt is as much a mineral poison as white paint.

I hear from everybody of the wonderful hot summer you have had. I suppose the grapes must have ripened out of doors this year in the south.[77] Did I ever tell you that I satisfied myself that the plant which grows over the house at Leicester is not poison ivy, tho' so like it that I had to examine closely—but the poison plant grows by little roots from the stalk, just as real ivy does, whilst the plant at the rectory sends out little finger-like tendrils on stalks—but the leaves are exactly alike. There was a Catalpa tree at Coloma with leaves nearly a foot across. Do you know the tree? There used to be a great many in the 'Place Verte' &c of German and Flemish towns when I was there, along with acacias, all trimmed and cropped.

Give my love to the little ones and tell them I caught a humming bird yesterday, and fed it with sugar and then let it go. It was not so large as my finger in its body. It came into the drawing-room.

Love to John.

Believe me

Your affectionate Mother-in-law
Catherine A. Hubback

41

October 8th [1876]
Oakland

My dear John,

I have heard from Charlie, who says he will be very glad to receive me as I propose. They hope to get into their house by the beginning of November and if I leave here so as to reach them by the 1st or 2nd December they will have had time enough to arrange themselves before I come. He thinks if he can leave Dina during the day he can get a good deal of work in the neighbourhood, but he does not like leaving her alone in that lonely place with the 3 children to look after and everything else besides: I intend when there, if possible, to have a European servant—a German girl to help in the house. It would be much better than 'colored persons' who are so idle and independent, and I don't fancy Irish girls would like such a situation, Germans or Swedes make the best servants.

I did not have any letter from you last week. I hope Mary continues to improve, I shall be very glad to hear that she is allowed to leave her bed. It must be very weakening lying in it.

The autumn rains are just threatening—we have had a slight shower or two, and the sky is very much broken up. We had an earthquake on Friday night too, about 9:20—but I could not get Edward to feel it, he heard the windows rattle, but though it lasted long enough for me to say, 'There's the earthquake,' and Edward said, 'Is it? I don't feel it—I heard the windows rattle,' and I said, 'Why it's going on still'—he could not feel it, and then it had done. It was just as if the house had been set going on rockers—no jerk, as is usual. I daresay we shall have another or two. It has been such a very fine summer, and hardly a storm of wind even—and no thunder at all, so there must be a balance of electricity due somewhere or other.

I have communicated to most of my acquaintance the interesting fact that I am going away, but oddly enough, nobody has ever suggested the idea that Edward is thinking of marrying, and as yet there are not six people who know that, I suppose they have got tired of thinking it, as they used to be always pairing him with somebody and finding out they were wrong.

This is Charlie's birthday, and he is 29 today.

I think I shall start on the 24th of November which would bring me to Chicago I suppose on a Tuesday or Wednesday. I don't want to be there on Sunday anyhow—the trains stop there, and it is so uncomfortable on Sunday of all days in the week, to be turned out in a strange town for 2 or 3 hours, and alone too. Do you know travelling dressing bags, like the one you gave me are quite novelties in this country, and mine is extremely admired? I shall have it with me on my journey I expect, as it is not so much beyond my power to lift now, as it was when I came, and I shall not be obliged to carry my eider down pillow, without which I could not have travelled last year. You must calculate about your letters, and not write to *me* here after the 2nd or 3rd of November but send a letter to reach Gainesville about 1st December—and write to Edward in the mean time here—you see if I were delayed in starting I should hear of you then, and if not it will be all right.

I want you to send me out a box by a Baltimore steamer. Pack up my coffee-pot and my books—my own which I left—and Scott's novels, and my 2 volumes of Macaulay's history, and any of Charlie's books you can find. They will be all old, so there will be no duty to pay, and Charlie has no books in Virginia—except a Tennyson and a Scott's poems—and a cookery book; if there

is room you can put in any of the shilling novels I left behind. If you send it out by a steamer which would reach Baltimore about the middle of December it will do—you will of course let us know when to expect it—but don't put in anything new, that there may be no trouble about duty.
Love to Mary and the girls—

Your affectionate Mother
Catherine A. Hubback

42

Oakland
October 29th [1876]

My dear Mary,

I am very glad that John was able to send an improving account of you, when he wrote from Wales, and also that he was having a little holiday. I have no doubt he wanted it.

I remember Raglan Castle very well, especially the beautiful terrace and trees round it. I think I went everywhere about it that was practicable and all round the outside of the walls as far as I could. I was there with a large pic-nic party, but crept about by myself over the ruins. The windows of the grand banquetting hall I think were very fine. The only room if I remember right was up in one of the gate-towers. It was besieged and taken in the civil wars—one of the sons, Lord Glamorgan, turning traitor. I am not sure about the father—was it the old Marquis of Worcester—or did he not defend Basing house? The name was Herbert, I have a notion—or was it the Seymour family? I daresay you could find something about it in the *Book of Days*.[78] Tell John to look it up and send me word, or I shall puzzle my brains about the siege, and I have no books of reference.

I suppose in your next letter you will say about my going to Virginia what you think of it. It seems likely that Edward will not leave Oakland—the Visalia business does not suit exactly. Perhaps Mr Hawes and Mr Sweet will find something else better for him. I am not sorry altogether, as it would have been a great risk in some respects. It makes no difference as to my movements, and I fully intend to go on the 24th if all is well then.

I am going to turn over the presidentship of the young ladies' society to a Mrs Fish, who is very popular with some of the members. and a very good person to manage it. *She* says she will make them work—I never could get most of them to do anything, the only thing they care for is the monthly social, to which no young ladies not members are admitted, and which has become so popular with a very nice set of young men now at Oakland that invitations are much sought after. The members have taken them in turn, and there is no expense or trouble, as a glass of lemonade is the only refreshment permitted. We have had several very pleasant evenings. The members subscribe $3 a year which goes to the Church Missions in California.

I mean to have a farewell social next month, to which I shall invite everybody I know—and sell off by a lottery of dollar tickets all the work I have in stock—some very pretty things—the larger part my own work. I expect to realise about 25 dollars, to hand over to the Mission fund and so take leave. The tickets will be all prizes.

Charlie is getting on fast with his new house. They want to get in in a week, and finish a great deal after they have moved. It has a room on each side of the entrance, which latter opens out at the back to the kitchen, and upstairs there are 3 rooms, besides the passage in the middle and a good store closet. It could easily be added to if desirable and as it has stood through a terrible storm it must be well built. The room I am to have has a southeast aspect, which I prefer. He will put up a veranda on the south side next spring—and I think the southeast end would be a very good one for a greenhouse if that is possible, not as a luxury for flowers however but to raise early vegetables and delicacies for the market.

It will be something quite new to me to live quite in the country—we have to walk a long way now to reach anything like country—Oakland grows so fast. Edward and I walked nearly 6 miles this afternoon—a long way down the wharf which runs out far into the bay—where the air was very fresh and pleasant.

We have had a cascade of rain, and the ground is hard, and the grass everywhere quite green   it is very early for it. I hope it will wash away some of the smallpox and diphtheria which has been prevalent and fatal amongst children here. I daresay it would be much worse in this flat place, where there is no wind, if it were not for the abundance of gum trees[79] which purify the air so much.

With love to you all
Believe me

Your affectionate Mother-in-law
Catherine A. Hubback

43

November 5th [1876]
Oakland

My dear Mary,

I was very glad to have your letter from Larchwood saying that you were improving. I have no doubt the change did you good. I do hope you will be careful of yourself, and not do too much at any time, so as to throw yourself back.

You may pity me for having to pull all the house to pieces, and leave California which I like so much, and go through so much labour in packing and settling everything here—but you need not pity me in the least for the journey. The necessary expense of course is an evil, but I am so fond of travelling for its own sake, that I assure you I do not dread that at all. The trains are so very much improved since I came out 6 years ago—and I am so much more used to the American style now, that I rather enjoy the idea of the journey—what I do mind is leaving Edward, and some other friends here, and I dread all the necessary labour of the next fortnight. During the whole journey until Washington is reached one only has to change trains twice, and that is the only uncomfortable part. Crossing the Missouri which one does in a small, uncomfortable train—and going from one station to another at Chicago. Of course I should like very well then to have a companion to help look after the baggage and secure tickets, but as I managed to get through when I was so weak and helpless I am not afraid now when I am perfectly able to exert myself. For the rest, one sits in one's section all day, and lies down at night, and listens to the complaints or worries of other people, at least I do, with philosophical amusement. At this time of year the cars going East are not so much crowded—and starting from this end, I shall probably meet with acquaintance, or make them.

I should mind leaving Edward a great deal more, if I saw more of him but his business so constantly takes him out at 6 o'clock and so often keeps him out till 8 or 9 that you see I have very long days, when I am no good to him—whilst in Virginia I shall have plenty to do for the others, and always companions when I want them. The dullest sort of life is having nobody but oneself to work for or please and when I have darned Edward's sock there seems to be nothing else to do for him. I quite think with pleasure of being useful again. There will be plenty of needle-work to do, and the children to teach and play with, and helping Dina in many ways, and by and by there will be gardening and lots of contrivances and things for my room and so forth. If the next 3 weeks were only over, I do feel sometimes like sitting down and crying merely at the number of things I have to arrange and look after.

If Edward can get some photos of Florence he says he will send you one, that you may see what an American girl is like. She is fair, with an immense quantity of light brown hair—not golden at all—and she is very like in air and general effect a great many other American girls. There is such a strong national resemblance amongst them all. It always surprises me when I think of it, that there should be, as the nation is so young, and the old families began with being English.

As she was not at a public school I suspect she is much better informed than most girls, they learn very little at all their great schools, so far as I can find out. Edith Akerly who is 11 years old, is only in long division and besides learning geography and history—everything else is extra and has to be learnt out of school hours and paid for—school hours being 3 in the forenoon and 2 in the afternoon—lessons to be learnt at home. I shall expect Carrie and Mary to be in long division by the time they are 9 at least—or they will not be worthy of their father. Needle-work American girls rarely learn at all until they leave school—so any English child is sure to beat them at that.

You may think of me as somewhere on the plains when you read this. America is convulsed by the Presidential election—I shall be glad when it is well over. One hardly knows what may come.

Love to John and the little ones

Your affectionate Mother-in-law

Catherine A. Hubback

44

December 26th [1876]
Gainesville

My dear Mary,

I was very glad to hear from your last letter that you were improving—though your progress is so slow, yet I hope it will be permanent.

We have rather an invalid house just now, as the children have bad colds, and baby has a tumour forming on his thigh poor child, which is very trying. I suppose it has something to do with teething—he is otherwise an extremely jolly and healthy child, and very good tempered when not in pain. We have uncommonly cold weather for the time of year, but it has not snowed much—and were it not that I have a bad foot, I could walk, which I have not done for a fortnight now. My boot hurt my heel and then the place took cold, and I have had a good deal of inflammation and poulticing to go through—and cannot yet put on a shoe or boot on my right foot. The heel is such an awkward place—one cannot walk without hurting it.

The place is beginning to look a little more finished. Some of the rubbish is cleared away, and Charlie has got all his fodder up, and some of the out-buildings—but he has a great deal to do still. A chicken house to build, and an out-of-door kitchen, and a barn and workshop—all the road to make, from the pike to the house, and all the garden and pastures to be laid out. Charlie has a nice pair of horses who do all the work, and I want him to get a strong waggon, which is to be sold for $50 in Haymarket, as he can then do all his own hauling lumber and stones, besides earn a good deal at spare times by hauling for other people. This would pay me for the waggon in the course of the year. I am not going to let him work out for other people until his own place is done. He had thought of taking a building contract, to raise money to finish his place. But I shall be able to supply funds to provide lumber, and then he can work at home. I shall not be satisfied until I see the place all put into *paying* condition.

Black women are horrid plagues in a house, but the men do work if they are overlooked—he has two who go with horses, and haul fodder, and milk and feed pigs—he has two cows now in milk, so we have plenty of cream, and are going to have butter, good butter, I mean. He killed 3 pigs last week for bacon, and sausage meat and he has a calf which will have to be eaten before long. We have been making mince meat last week—but one is badly off this year for apples. The frost has caught them all.

Edward wrote me word that he was very busy again. Things have taken a new start; and even thanksgiving day he got no holiday. That seems very long ago to me however. I was at Pittsburgh on thanksgiving day; and I don't care for it the least—it is only a day on which patriotic Americans stuff themselves with turkey and pumpkin pies, and their nasty mince pies, which are so gross they make one sick—and have the effrontery to compare their occupation of this country to the children of Israel in Canaan. To be sure so far as exterminating the original inhabitants they are something alike.

People here—I mean in the States, expect a great out-break about the President—as there is no doubt Tilden has the majority,[80] but Grant declares he shall not have it; and that he will keep him out by force; so there is likely to be more trouble—and they still have a heavy Indian war in store for next year—and it takes ten soldiers to each Indian to make a favorable result certain—the redmen are so much the best soldiers.

I wish you all a happy Xmas and New Year. It is long since I have seen a wintry Xmas—they have flowers and sunshine I have no doubt in California unless it is wet.

My love to you all—

Your affectionate Mother-in-law

Catherine A. Hubback

12 *Sacramento Railroad Station* is the work of William Hahn (1829–87), who was born in Germany and came to California in 1872. His adept rendering of clothing would have appealed to Catherine, who may have seen this painting exhibited in San Francisco in 1874. (*Fine Arts Museums of San Francisco, Museum purchase, M. H. de Young Endowment Fund, 54936*)

EPILOGUE

Catherine Hubback died in Gainesville, Virginia, on 25 February 1877, and was interred in the burial ground of St Paul's Episcopal Church in nearby Haymarket. She was fifty-eight years old. The grave marker is inscribed 'In Memory of Catherine, wife of John Hubback of the Inner Temple, London, England,' followed by a verse from Psalm 107: 'Then are they glad because they are at rest, and so he bringeth them unto the haven where they would be.' She died of pneumonia, according to the death certificate, for which information was supplied by her son Charles. Her marital status was recorded as 'unmarried.'

Edward Hubback married Florence Bentley in December 1877. They lived in Oakland and Alameda, changing houses five times in fifteen years, as Edward moved from job to job in San Francisco, working mostly as a shipping clerk. In 1892 Florence died after giving birth to their sixth child. She was thirty-six years old and was buried in the Bentley family plot at Mountain View Cemetery. The children were dispersed, and no record of their father can be found until 1900, when the census lists him as a farm laborer in Santa Cruz County, boarding with a large Italian family. He appears in the 1920 census as a wood-chopper. He died on a ranch in El Dorado County in December 1924, aged seventy-eight, and was buried in Auburn.

Charles Hubback and his wife Bernhardine had six children, of whom two survived to adulthood. In 1881 the family moved to San Jose, California, where they occupied a dozen houses over forty years. Charles worked for the Santa Clara Valley Mill and Lumber Company for more than twenty years, primarily as a draftsman. He died at the age of seventy-six in April 1924, predeceasing Edward by eight months. His brother was living with him and Bernhardine at the time and was the informant for the death certificate. Charles's birth year is recorded as 1848 instead of 1847, and his father as 'unknown.'

John and Mary Hubback and their four young daughters left Rock Ferry six months after Catherine's death. They moved south to Lower Bebington and settled in a larger house, called Oak Lawn, where another daughter and two sons were born. John traveled widely in his work—eleven trips to Russia and twelve to Argentina—but he never returned to North America. He published three books about the grain trade and collaborated with his daughter Edith on *Jane Austen's Sailor Brothers* (1906). He left extensive memoirs, completing the last a year before his death in 1939, aged ninety-five.

MEMBERS OF THE AUSTEN FAMILY
MENTIONED IN THE LETTERS

As noted in the Introduction, Catherine Hubback belonged to a large family. Her father Francis Austen was one of eight children and begat eleven with his first wife, Mary Gibson, who died in 1823. His second wife, Martha Lloyd Austen, to whom Catherine refers as 'my Mother' in the letters, died in 1843. A well-connected woman of modest means, she had some years earlier received a legacy of £1,500 from a childless cousin. She bequeathed a portion to Catherine, who invested it in Edward's ill-fated partnership.

By the time Catherine moved to California in 1871, six of her siblings had died. References to the remaining four appear in the letters. Also mentioned are six of her fourteen nieces and nephews and the surviving spouses of a sister and brother. Of Catherine's thirty-odd first cousins, twelve were alive in 1871, of whom three figure in the letters.

SIBLINGS AND THEIR OFFSPRING

Frances Sophia Austen (1821–1904), called Fanny, never married. She kept house for her father at Portsdown Lodge until his death in 1865, when she moved to her brother Edward's rectory in Kent. Upon the death of his wife in childbirth in 1867, she assumed the care of his infant daughter and her sisters.

George Thomas Austen (1812–1903) attended Winchester College and St John's College, Oxford. He served until 1848 as a chaplain in the Royal Navy, and from 1856 to 1897 as rector of St John's Church, Redhill, four miles from Portsdown Lodge. In 1851 he married Louisa Tragett, to whose mother Catherine refers disparagingly. Two of his sons appear in the letters: **Francis George Heathcote (1857–85)** and **Ernest Leigh (1858–1939)**. Six of Jane Austen's letters to her brother Frank descended to the latter in 1904, upon the death of his aunt Fanny. He gave them to the British Museum in the 1930s.

Herbert Grey Austen (1815–88) was remembered by his nephew John as the uncle who took the most interest in him and his brothers and encouraged them at cricket. A commander in the Royal Navy, he married Louisa Lyns in 1863 and retired the following year to Whitley Lodge, Berkshire. Its proximity to Reading caused Catherine to refer to his daughters **Alice Mary (1863–1945)** and **Ella Frances (1865–1935)** as the 'Reading little girls.'

Janet Rose Austen (1856–1946) was the eldest daughter of Catherine's younger brother **Edward Thomas Austen (1820–1908)**, who attended St John's College, Oxford, and served fifty-three years as rector of the Church of St Nicholas, Barfreston, Kent.

Helen Catherine Purvis (b. 1835) was a daughter of Catherine's eldest sister Mary Jane, who died before Helen's second birthday. Her father, **George Thomas Maitland Purvis**, was the brother-in-law who inspired Catherine's 1872 observation that 'almost all family quarrels originate in money transactions.'

COUSINS

Frances Palmer Austen (1812–82) was Catherine's sister-in-law as well as her cousin. She was a daughter of Admiral Charles Austen, younger brother to Catherine's father. In 1842 she married Catherine's brother Francis, a captain in the Royal Navy, who died in 1858. She was called Fanny Frank, in order to distinguish her from Catherine's sister.

James Edward Austen-Leigh (1798–1874), called Edward, and his half-sister **Anna Austen Lefroy (1793–1872)** were children of Frank's eldest brother James. They belonged to the senior cohort of Jane Austen's nieces and nephews, had known their aunt well, and were adults at the time of Catherine's birth in 1818. This generational divide, common in large families, may account for Edward's reluctance to accept Catherine's contribution to his *Memoir* (see Introduction) and his failure to send her a copy of the second edition (see Letters 2, 3, and 5). He may also have been influenced by his half-sister, whose mistrust of 'Mrs Hubback' was icily conveyed to him in a letter in 1862.[1] Anna herself had had literary aspirations. A novel begun in 1812 received warm encouragement from her aunt, but was set aside and the manuscript destroyed in the 1830s. She published a novella and two children's stories and attempted a completion of a work left unfinished by Jane Austen and later known as 'Sanditon.' The success of her much younger cousin Catherine in turning another fragment, called 'The Watsons,' into a novel and following it with nine more in quick succession, may have embittered her.

Other Persons Mentioned
in the Letters

Unless otherwise noted, the persons cited resided in Oakland and were Americans born east of the Mississippi River.

Akerly: The Reverend Benjamin Akerly was named rector of St John's Episcopal Church in 1858. He and his wife Catherine lived with their seven children at 16th and Adeline Streets.

Alden: S. E. Alden and his wife Anna lived two miles north of downtown Oakland on a large property bordering Temescal Creek. Their daughter Elsie may have been the Miss Alden that Catherine mentions as a prospective second wife for John Wedderspoon. Mr Alden was a vestryman of St John's Episcopal Church.

Bacon: Ella Bacon and her sister Corinne were the daughters of Henry Bacon, a banker and real-estate broker, and his wife Julia. They owned a large home on Oak Street, just north of the Kirkham family. Ella Bacon married Frank Soulé, professor of civil engineering at the University of California and a vestryman of St John's Episcopal Church.

Bentley: Florence Cooper Bentley, born in 1856, lived with her widowed mother Marguerite at 1168 18th Street. Her father was U. S. Army Captain H. H. Bentley. She married Edward Hubback on 20 December 1877 (see Epilogue).

Blair: David Blair, born in Scotland, was a commission merchant in San Francisco. He married Leila Kirkham in 1872. Between 1875 and 1877 he obtained and lost a concession from the Mexican government to build a railway from Guaymas to the northern frontier of Sonora. He died in South Africa in the early 1880s.

Bowen: W. F. Bowen was a retired sea captain who in 1853 opened a roadhouse at what later became the northwest corner of Delaware Street and San Pablo Avenue in Berkeley. It evolved into a grocery and feed store and served stagecoaches running from Oakland.

Brotherton: George and Lewis Brotherton were check forgers who escaped from custody shortly after their conviction. They were recaptured and sent to San Quentin Prison.

Carr: In 1869 Ezra Carr was appointed professor of agriculture at the newly chartered University of California. His embattled tenure ended in dismissal in 1874. His wife Jeanne, née Smith, is notable for her long friendship with the naturalist John Muir. When her husband was elected superintendent of public instruction in 1875, he named her his deputy.

Emerson: D. L. Emerson, a real-estate agent, owned the house at 11th and Grove Streets where Catherine and Edward lived from 1871 to 1873. His brother Ralph Emerson, a carpenter, lived next door with his English wife Blanche.

Englekin: Bernhardine Englekin was born in Germany in 1852. She married Charles Hubback in 1871 (see Epilogue).

Fair: In 1870 Laura Fair fatally shot her lover Alexander Crittenden onboard the ferryboat *El Capitan*, in the presence of his wife and children. She was sentenced to be hanged, but a stay of execution resulted in a second trial and acquittal in 1872.

Foss: Clark Foss operated a stagecoach line from Calistoga to the Geysers. He earned an international reputation for his daring as a driver.

De Fremery: Adèle de Fremery and her brothers James and Florent, born in California, were the children of James de Fremery, born in the Netherlands of Huguenot stock, and his wife Virginie. In 1849 he came to San Francisco, where he prospered as a liquor importer. He served thirty years as consul for the Netherlands and was a vestryman of St John's Episcopal Church. He acquired nine acres in West Oakland and built a twenty-four-room house at 1621 Adeline Street. Family members, including Adèle and her husband, Pieter van Löben Sels, lived there until 1911, when it became the property of the City of Oakland. It survives as a recreation center.

Friedlander: Isaac Friedlander, born in Germany, came to California in the Gold Rush of 1849 but made his fortune in wheat. As production increased in the 1860s, he was a key developer of the export trade to Great Britain.

Goodwin: William Goodwin was a Liverpool grain trader and a friend of John Hubback.

Gurnett: W. J. Gurnett was a partner in the firm of Irwin, Gurnett & Co., specializing in furniture and bedding, at 12th Street and Broadway.

Hassell: James Hassell, born in England, was an accountant at the British Bank of North America in San Francisco.

Havens: In the 1870s Frank Havens was a San Francisco bank teller, boarding at Kelsey House. By the turn of the century, he controlled 13,000 acres in the Oakland hills and had founded both a streetcar network (later known as the Key System) and a water company to serve the growing population. He fostered the incorporation in 1907 of the city of Piedmont, where his home, designed by Bernard Maybeck, still stands, and an elementary school bears his name.

Heath: John Heath was a London barrister and the elder John Hubback's legal representative. He administered all the assets of the marriage, including Catherine's legacy from her stepmother.

Heatley: Edward D. Heatley, born in England, was a partner at Dickson, DeWolf, & Co., commission merchants, where Edward Hubback worked as a clerk.

Henderson: David Henderson, born in Scotland, was a bookkeeper who served as treasurer of St John's Episcopal Church.

Herd: John and Emma Herd and their five daughters were born in England. Mr Herd was a grain broker in San Francisco.

Holderness: Harold Holderness, born in England, was a commission merchant in San Francisco. He boarded briefly with Catherine, occupying Edward's room while the latter was in England. He moved to Alameda and boarded with Moses and George Cobb, attorneys, on High Street.

Hudson: Henry and Mary Hudson, both born in England, were Catherine and Edward's neighbors on 11th Street. Mr Hudson was a merchant in San Francisco.

Jordan: Joseph Jordan and his family were Catherine and Edward's next-door neighbors on Grove Street, succeeding the Emersons in 1872. Mr Jordan was a merchant in San Francisco and a vestryman of St John's Episcopal Church.

Keith: William Keith, born in Scotland, was a prolific painter, noted in the 1870s for panoramic landscapes of the Sierra Nevada. His subject matter was influenced by his friendship with John Muir, to whom he was introduced by Jeanne Carr.

Kelsey: Wright Kelsey and his wife owned a substantial property on the west side of Telegraph Avenue near Sycamore Street. Mrs Kelsey managed the boarding establishment of Kelsey House and Cottages, while her husband operated a horticultural nursery.

Kirkham: Leila Kirkham, born in Missouri, was the eldest daughter of Brigadier General Ralph Kirkham and his wife Catherine. Her sisters Kate and May also figure in the letters. Their parents were prominent members of St John's Episcopal Church, where General Kirkham was senior warden. Mrs Kirkham was a founder of Oakland's first hospital. Their home at 8th and Oak Street was one of several large properties lining the estuary: a neighborhood now occupied by Laney College and the Lake Merritt BART station.

In 1872 Leila Kirkham married David Blair, who died in the early 1880s. In 1886 she married an Englishman, the Hon. Walter Yarde-Buller, who declared bankruptcy two years later. The troubled marriage ended in divorce in 1896. She returned to California in 1900 and was committed by her sister May to a sanitarium, where she died in 1904.

Knox: Israel Knox was an iron founder in San Francisco and a member of the Oakland City Council. He and his wife Rebecca owned a tract of land on the west side of Telegraph Avenue, north of the Kelsey property. Mrs Knox ran a boarding house, called Knox House, where John and Edward Hubback stayed in 1868.

Laidlaw: Walter and Elizabeth Laidlaw were both born in England. Mr Laidlaw was a bookkeeper in San Francisco and later a lumber dealer in Oakland.

Lemon: Josephine Lemon was a teacher at Peralta School, a one-room building on Alcatraz Avenue.

Makin: Edward Hubback's unscrupulous partner Robert Makin, born in England, was a member of a prominent grain-trading family in Liverpool. His wife Rebecca, also born in England, was a daughter of James Ross, who in 1857 acquired 8,877 acres in Marin County. The town of Ross, incorporated in 1908, was named in his honor. The Makins maintained a home in San Francisco, but their primary residence was with Rebecca's widowed mother Anna in San Rafael.

Marsh: Maria and Lillie Marsh were the daughters of E. Marsh, a printer, and his wife Lillie. They were classmates of Kate Kirkham at Mrs Poston's Seminary for Young Ladies on Oak Street, now the site of the Oakland Museum of California.

Morse: G. D. Morse operated a photography studio at 417 Montgomery Street, San Francisco.

Oxland: Charles Oxland, born in England, was a clerk in San Francisco and served as treasurer of St John's Episcopal Church.

Riley: The two Miss Rileys were the daughters of B. F. Riley, a commission merchant and liquor importer born in England. The family boarded at Kelsey House.

Segar: Halsall Segar was the senior partner at Segar & Tunicliffe, grain traders, when John Hubback joined the Liverpool firm in 1869. Upon his death in 1873, he was succeeded by his younger son Edward. His elder son Halsall became a clergyman.

Seymour: In 1849 Catherine, in search of a cure for her husband, took the family to the home of her friends Edward and Elizabeth Seymour in the Welsh village of Llanelli, near Abergavenny.

Smith: Stephen Smith served St John's Episcopal Church as a vestryman and as Sunday School superintendent.

Thorniewell: Edward Thorniewell succeeded Halsall Segar as senior partner at Segar & Tunnicliffe, grain traders.

Turner: The Reverend Charles Turner, rector of St Paul's Episcopal Church, lived at the Tubbs Hotel in the Brooklyn section of Oakland.

Watkins: Carleton Watkins (1829–1916) was one of the most prolific and influential photographers of his era. At the time of Catherine's consignment, his Yosemite Gallery was located at 429 Montgomery Street, San Francisco.

Wedderspoon: John and Thomas Wedderspoon, both born in Scotland, were commission merchants at the firm of Cross & Cross in San Francisco. They lived on Myrtle Street near the house occupied by Catherine and Edward in 1876.

Williams: Henry Williams was curate of St Mark's, Catherine's church in the parish of Bebington, Cheshire.

Woolsey: Miss M. L. Woolsey was the daughter of E. W. Woolsey, an insurance agent in San Francisco, and his wife

Martha. The family boarded at Kelsey House in the 1870s and later moved to Berkeley.

PLACES OF INTEREST
MENTIONED IN THE LETTERS

Unless otherwise noted, the places cited are in California.

The **Adelphi Hotel** in Liverpool catered to transatlantic steamship passengers. Its counterpart in New York was the Brevoort.

Alameda, now an island off the Oakland waterfront, was a peninsula until 1901, when a cut was made to facilitate shipping.

Barfreston is a hamlet in Kent, eight miles south-east of Canterbury. The twelfth-century church of St Nicholas, where Catherine's brother Edward was rector, is renowned for its Norman architecture and luxuriant carvings.

Brayton Hall was the principal building of the College of California. The six-block campus extended from Franklin to Harrison Streets, bounded by 12th and 14th Streets.

Broadway is the primary north-east–south-west thoroughfare in Oakland, terminating at the waterfront.

The **Calaveras Big Trees** are fifty miles north-west of Yosemite Valley. The giant sequoias (*Sequoia gigantea*) were a popular tourist destination in Catherine's time, but there is no evidence that she traveled there.

Calistoga lies at the head of the Napa Valley, an area long known to native people for its mineral springs. It was developed as a resort in the 1860s, and its contemporary appeal is enhanced by the proximity of more than thirty wineries.

Chawton House, Catherine's birthplace, was built in the seventeenth century on land acquired in 1551 by John Knight. In 1781 it passed to Thomas Knight, who, with his wife Catherine Knatchbull, adopted Catherine's uncle Edward Austen; Edward inherited Chawton House in 1812 and took the surname Knight. In 1826, four years after the departure of Catherine Austen's family, it became the home of Edward's eldest son, also Edward, who fathered sixteen children there and died in 1879. It is to his second wife, Adela Portal, that Catherine refers in 1872.

Successive heirs struggled to maintain the property until 1993, when a 125-year lease was acquired by a charity founded by Sandy Lerner, an American philanthropist. Substantial restoration work ensued, and the house reopened in 2003 as Chawton House Library, a center for study and research in early English women's writing.

Cheltenham, Gloucestershire, was famous for its spa, which was visited in 1816 by Jane and Cassandra Austen. Edward and Charles Hubback attended Cheltenham College, founded in 1841.

Christ Church was established in Alameda in 1871 and moved in 1896 to its current site at Grand Street and Santa Clara Avenue. The church was served by several English rectors.

The **Cliff House** of Catherine's day was built in 1863 on the westernmost promontory of San Francisco and offered fine dining with a spectacular view. Southbound steamships passed close enough for passengers to discern the faces of friends waving farewell from the terrace. This structure and its successor were destroyed by fire. The current building dates to 1909.

Coloma was the first of the Gold Rush towns, owing to its proximity to John Sutter's mill, where gold was discovered in 1848.

Dupont Street, laid out in 1845 as Calle de la Fundación and renamed Grant Avenue in 1906, is the oldest street in San Francisco. The blocks between Bush Street and Broadway traverse the heart of Chinatown.

Gainesville, Virginia, lies one mile south-east of Haymarket and eight miles west of Bull Run, a battle site of the American Civil War. In 1862 Gainesville served as a staging area for the Federal army, which lost 14,000 men. Confederate losses were 10,000.

The volcanic terrain known as '**The Geysers**' lies seventy miles north of San Francisco in the Mayacamas mountains of Sonoma and Lake Counties. The name is a misnomer, as the area is characterized, not by geysers, but by fumaroles: vents emitting steam derived from groundwater heated by magma. This phenomenon, known for millennia to the native people, began drawing visitors in the 1840s. By the time of the Hubbacks' visit, it was the vertiginous journey itself that was the main attraction. The excursion Catherine describes followed a popular itinerary: entry from the west by way of Healdsburg or Cloverdale, a stay at the Geysers Resort Hotel, and a high-speed exit via Pine Tree Flat and Calistoga.

Efforts to harness the steam for commercial purposes began in the 1920s. By the turn of the century, the thirty-square-mile site had become the world's largest complex of geothermal power plants.

The **Giant's Causeway**, a promontory on the north coast of County Antrim, Northern Ireland, is notable for its hexagonal columns of basalt. There is no evidence that Catherine traveled there, but images were widely available.

Golden Gate Park was in an early stage of development when the Hubbacks explored it in a rented buggy. The unpromising tract of sand dunes stretched three miles from the Pacific Ocean to the outskirts of settled San Francisco. Reclamation had begun with the planting of trees, including thousands of eucalyptus, Monterey pine, and Monterey cypress.

Grove Street, renamed Martin Luther King Jr Way in 1984, runs north-east from the waterfront, linking Oakland and Berkeley.

Half-moon Bay is the name given by American settlers to both 'Spanish Town' and its setting: a four-mile stretch of San Mateo County coastline, twenty-three miles south of San Francisco. 'Spanish Town' was a nickname for the Mexican settlement of San Benito. The name was changed in 1862 to Half-moon Bay and in 1905 to Half Moon Bay.

Haymarket, Virginia, sustained heavy damage in the American Civil War. Fires set by Federal troops in 1862 spared four buildings, including St Paul's Episcopal Church, where Catherine was buried in 1877.

Holy Trinity Church, at the corner of Albany and Euston Streets, was the Hubbacks' church when they lived in Torrington Square, Bloomsbury.

Huyton, an eastern suburb of Liverpool, was the home of John Hubback's senior partner Halsall Segar and his wife.

Lake Tahoe, on California's border with Nevada, drew few vacationers until the 1890s. Catherine's impression may have come from Samuel Clemens (Mark Twain), whose account of a camping trip to the mountain lake appeared in his 1872 book *Roughing It*.

Larchwood, Rock Ferry, was the home of P. T. Hall and his wife, neighbors and friends of John and Mary Hubback.

Leamington, Warwickshire, was known for its saline springs. The pump room and baths drew distinguished visitors, including Queen Victoria. In 1838, by royal license, the resort was named Royal Leamington Spa.

Leicester, the county town of Leicestershire, was a center for brewing and manufacturing. Mary Hubback's mother moved there in 1874, when her son William Clavell Ingram was appointed vicar of St Matthew's Church.

Liskeard is a town in Cornwall, just off the southern edge of Bodmin Moor.

Llangollen, set in a gorge cut by the Dee River, was a popular tourist gateway to northern Wales. Railway service to Ruabon, connecting with the Chester and Birkenhead line, made the journey feasible for Mary Hubback, traveling with small children.

Malvern is both a town in the Malvern Hills, south-west of Worcester, and a name applied to a group of settlements known for the healing properties of 'Malvern Water.' The area began drawing large numbers of spa visitors in the 1840s, especially to Great Malvern, the historic center and the site of Dr Wilson's Hydropathic Establishment, where Catherine brought her family in 1848.

Market Street is the primary east–west thoroughfare in San Francisco, beginning at the ferry landing on the bay.

Mills Seminary, founded in 1852 as the Young Ladies Seminary of Benicia, was established on the outskirts of Oakland in 1871. In 1885 it was chartered as Mills College.

Mount Diablo rises 3,864 feet in Contra Costa County, at the western edge of the Central Valley. With no comparable peaks in its vicinity, it can be seen from much of northern California, including San Francisco, thirty miles to the west. Two roads opened in May 1874, six weeks before Catherine's birthday visit.

The **Needles** are a jagged chalk formation at the western tip of the Isle of Wight.

Ocean House, four miles south-west of San Francisco proper, rewarded visitors to its remote location with views of Lake Merced and the Pacific, as well as recreation in the form of billiards and bowling. The Hubbacks, in a one-horse buggy, drove there on a toll road that followed present-day Upper Market Street and Portola Drive.

Pescadero, two miles inland from the southern San Mateo coast, attracted wheat and barley farmers in the 1850s. A significant number were New Englanders, and their building style was Classical Revival. A good example was the popular Swanton House, where Catherine and her friends, the MacCanns, apparently failed to make reservations. As its name implies, the town's initial appeal to visitors derived from the abundance of trout in Pescadero Creek. By the 1870s tourists were attracted by the 'pebbles': sand-polished fragments of topaz, carnelian, jasper, and the like.

The new lighthouse, to which the exasperating Mrs Boston diverted the traveling party, was built at Pigeon Point, five miles south of Pescadero. Its Fresnel lens was first illuminated six months after Catherine's visit.

Raglan Castle, Monmouthshire, begun in 1435, was the last medieval fortress built in Britain.

Redhill, Havant, Hampshire, was the home of Catherine's brother George, who served for forty years as rector of St John's Church.

Sacramento, at the junction of the Sacramento and American Rivers, became the capital of California in 1854.

St John's Episcopal Church was built on land donated by Ralph Kirkham. It occupied the corner of 8th and Grove Streets from 1859 until the 1950s, when the congregation moved to Gouldin Road in the Montclair district.

St Mary of the Immaculate Conception Church stands today on a brick foundation laid in 1868 at the corner of 8th and Jefferson Streets. Owing to a severe earthquake in October of that year, wood replaced the intended brick in the building's construction. The spires planned for the towers that Catherine mentions were never built. When the Diocese of Oakland was created in 1962, a more imposing church, St Francis de Sales, was designated its first cathedral. St Mary's congregation dwindled into the 1980s, when the church was slated for closure. In 1989 its fate was altered again by an earthquake, which left the church intact but damaged the cathedral beyond repair. St Mary's absorbed the latter's congregation and held services until 2008, when the building was closed upon completion of the Cathedral of Christ the Light.

St Paul's Episcopal Church was founded in 1871 at 12th and Webster Streets. In 1880 it moved to 14th and Harrison Streets and in 1912 to its present location at Montecito and Grand Avenues.

The **San Joaquin Valley** is the southern portion of the Central Valley, extending east from the coastal mountains to the Sierra Nevada and south from Stockton to Bakersfield. Its importance as a source of dry-land wheat declined in the 1870s, as the transcontinental railroad and the advent of irrigation made crops like fruit more profitable.

San Jose and **Santa Clara** trace their origins to 1777, when colonists from Mexico established Pueblo de San José de Guadalupe, and the Franciscan order founded Mission de Santa Clara de Asís. By 1870 the pueblo was a city of 9,000, and its neighbor a small town. The former mission site was acquired by Santa Clara College, founded by the Jesuit order in 1851, and renamed Santa Clara University in 1985. The two communities were connected by the Alameda, a four-mile road shaded by willow trees. A horse-drawn streetcar line was established in 1868.

San Mateo was established in 1793 as an outpost of Mission Dolores, twenty miles to the north in San Francisco. Railroad service between the cities began in 1863 and encouraged wealthy San Franciscans to build second homes in San Mateo County.

San Pablo Road originated in the Spanish colonial era as the 'road of the opposite coast.' It connected the waterfront with Rancho San Pablo and took that name in 1853, when Contra Costa County was divided, creating Alameda County. It ran north from Oakland along present-day San Pablo Avenue.

Santa Cruz, at the northern edge of Monterey Bay, was a
bustling resort by the time of Catherine's visit. A boardwalk
was in place, a luxury hotel offered roller-skating as well as
tennis and croquet, and the Dolphin Baths featured hot salt-
water plunges accompanied by calliope music.

Saucelito (from the Spanish *sauce*, willow), was the original
name of San Francisco's nearest neighbor, Sausalito, two
miles to the north in Marin County. Access via the Golden
Gate was limited to boat owners until the early 1870s,
when a ferry service was established. Both spellings were
used until 1897, when the postal designation was changed
to 'Sausalito.'

The **Sierra Nevada** ('snow-covered mountain range') extends
four hundred miles along California's eastern border and
was first surveyed in the 1860s.

Teignmouth is a seaside resort in Devon, perhaps visited by
Jane Austen when she and Cassandra and their parents stayed
up the coast in Dawlish in 1802.

Telegraph Road was built along a telegraph line from
downtown Oakland to the eastern hills. The segment from
Broadway to the city limits followed the route of present-day
Telegraph Avenue and carried the city's first horse-drawn
streetcars. The line was extended in 1873 to serve the
University of California.

The **University of California** was chartered in 1868.
It combined state-mandated instruction in mining and
agriculture with the liberal arts curriculum of its forerunner,
the College of California. By 1873 members of the faculty
were commuting to a new campus five miles to the north:
160 hillside acres along Strawberry Creek. The sparsely

populated area was named in honor of the Anglo-Irish Bishop George Berkeley, whose poem 'Destiny of America' includes the line: 'Westward the course of empire takes its way.'

Vallejo, at the mouth of the Napa River, was a naval and commercial hub as well as a transfer point for travelers. A ferry terminal connecting to railway lines provided regular service from 1869 until 1937, when traffic shifted to bridges. Ferry operations resumed in 1986 and continue today, having received a boost in 1989, when earthquake damage closed the San Francisco–Oakland Bay Bridge for a month.

Virginia City, Nevada, owed its prosperity to the Comstock Lode, where gold and silver were discovered in 1859. John Hubback traveled there in 1868.

Watsonville, five miles inland from Monterey Bay, was well established as an agricultural center by 1871, when the arrival of the railroad made it a gateway to the tourist destinations of Santa Cruz and Pescadero.

White Sulphur Springs, two miles west of St Helena in a narrow canyon cut by Sulphur Creek, was the Napa Valley's first thermal resort. A hotel that opened in 1852 was the first of many buildings to succumb to fire, but by the 1870s the location was well regarded as a watering place for wealthy San Franciscans. Its decline began toward the end of the nineteenth century, as a succession of owners ran it under different names, and at varying levels of respectability. It reassumed its original name in 1983 and operated as a spa until 2007.

Yosemite Valley, 150 miles due east of San Francisco, was a primary destination in Catherine's time. John wrote a charming account of his visit there in 1868, but there is no evidence that his mother ever made the trip.

NOTES

The objective of the notes is twofold: to define obscure terms, literary references, and historical events; and to clarify ambiguous references to people and places. Members of the Austen family are identified on pages 177–9, other persons mentioned in the letters on pages 181–8, and places on pages 189–98.

Introduction

1 *The Younger Sister* (1850), *The Wife's Sister, or The Forbidden Marriage* (1851), *Life and Its Lessons* (1851), *May and December* (1854), *Malvern, or The Three Marriages* (1855), *The Old Vicarage* (1856), *Agnes Milbourne* (1856), *The Rival Suitors* (1857), *The Stage and the Company* (1858), *The Mistakes of a Life* (1863).
2 *The Younger Sister* (London, 1850), p. ii.
3 *The Old Vicarage* (London, 1856), p. 15.
4 Ibid., p. 9.
5 Cassandra Austen to Philadelphia Walter, 14 February 1827, quoted by Maggie Lane, *Jane Austen's Family through Five Generations* (London, 1984), p. 207.
6 John Hubback, unpublished typescript (1938), p. 19.
7 Cassandra Austen to Philadelphia Walter, 20 January 1832, quoted by Maggie Lane, p. 219.
8 *Life and Its Lessons* (London, 1851).
9 Jane Austen to Cassandra Austen, 13 October 1808, *Jane Austen's Letters*, p. 147.
10 Jane Leigh Perrot to James Edward Austen, quoted by Maggie Lane, p. 208.

11 Francis W. Austen, unpublished memoir, quoted by Maggie Lane, p. 218.

12 Sir Francis Austen to William Knight, unpublished letter (*c.*1860), Austen-Leigh family collection, 23M93/86/3b/64/3, Hampshire Record Office, Winchester.

13 Two of Frank's older brothers had held these scholarships, which were awarded to those who could prove kinship with Sir Thomas White, the founder of the college. The line of descent was through their mother, Cassandra Leigh. The practice was abolished by Act of Parliament in 1861.

14 Hopkinson deposit, Jane Austen's House Museum, Chawton.

15 Knight Commander of the Order of the Bath.

16 Hopkinson deposit, Jane Austen's House Museum, Chawton.

17 *The Wife's Sister, or The Forbidden Marriage* (London, 1851); *May and December* (London, 1854).

18 The 832-page treatise was published in 1844. The preface acknowledges Catherine's brother Henry: 'Among the friends to whom I am indebted, I must name Mr Austen, of the Chancery Bar . . .'

19 The book, published in 1842, was Dr Wilson's response to criticism from his fellow physicians. Having rejected conventional drug treatments, he advocated hydropathy: the treatment of disease by bathing in and drinking water. He prescribed a regime of wet sheets, hot baths, and cold showers, combined with vigorous exercise. Malvern, with its hills and springs, was an ideal setting.

20 *The Mistakes of a Life* (London, 1863).

21 John Hubback, unpublished typescript (1938), p. 46.

22 Ibid., p. 38.

23 Catherine Hubback to Mary Ingram, unpublished letter (1867), MS. Eng. c. 7100, fols 31–9 Bodleian Library.

24 John Hubback, *Cross Currents in a Long Life*, privately printed (1935), p. 14.

25 Edward Hubback to Catherine Hubback, unpublished letter (1868), MS. Eng. c. 7100, fols 62–71 Bodleian Library.

26 John Hubback, unpublished typescript (1938), p. 54.

27 Ibid , p. 20,

28 R. W. Chapman, *Jane Austen: Facts and Problems* (Oxford: The Clarendon Press, 1949), p. 62. Correspondence on the *Memoir* was gathered in a volume which descended to James Edward's grandson Richard Arthur Austen-Leigh, who showed it to Dr Chapman in the 1920s and apparently kept it at his apartment in Albany Street, London, which was heavily damaged by bombing during the Second World War.

29 John Hubback, unpublished typescript (1938), p. 56.

30 Ibid., p. 62.

The Letters

1 The fair raised $34,000 for the Mechanics Institute, founded in 1854 as a center for adult technical education.

2 Probably a reference to London's Great Exhibition of 1851, which John had attended with his uncle Joseph Hubback.

3 Wells Fargo & Company opened in San Francisco in the wake of the Gold Rush, offering banking and express delivery service to miners and merchants. From 1866 to the completion of the Transcontinental Railroad in 1869, it monopolized long-distance overland transportation in the western United States.

4 Probably an abalone shell.

5 *Sequoia sempervirens* (coast redwood).

6 Mrs Norris, the insufferable aunt in Jane Austen's novel *Mansfield Park*, avoids making a home for her niece Fanny

Price by claiming she 'must keep a spare room for a friend.'

7 *Lady Susan* is the title given by James Edward Austen-Leigh to a short novel completed by Jane Austen *c*.1795 and set aside. It was first published in 1871, when he included it in the second edition of his *Memoir of Jane Austen*. The spine bears the inscription 'Lady Susan &.'

8 See Austen, Frances Sophia.

9 See Austen, Frances Palmer.

10 Stoneleigh Abbey, Warwickshire, was acquired in 1561 by Sir Thomas Leigh, Lord Mayor of London. Catherine's paternal grandmother, Cassandra Leigh (1739–1827), was related to three potential heirs to Stoneleigh, who resolved their claims in 1806. Ownership passed to Cassandra's first cousin, the Reverend Thomas Leigh, and his nephew, James Leigh, who together bought out Cassandra's brother, James Leigh-Perrot. He was the great-uncle to whom Catherine refers. The transaction, a profitable one for him and his wife, was nonetheless resented in the immediate family. Seven years afterwards, Jane Austen referred to it as a 'vile compromise' in a letter to Catherine's father, Francis Austen.

11 See Austen, Herbert Grey.

12 See St John's Episcopal Church.

13 Kirk Michael, Isle of Man, where Mary Hubback's elder brother, the Reverend William Ingram, and her mother Jane Ingram had settled in 1865.

14 Perhaps a reference to arrowroot: *Maranta arundinnacea*, a tropical American plant. Starch from its roots was used by native people to absorb poison from arrow wounds.

15 See Christ Church.

16 Probably a song by Charles Gounod (1818–93). It was common in the nineteenth century for sacred songs by

well-known composers to make their way into the worship service.

17 'The Stewardess' Story' by Mrs C. Austen Hubback opens as a transatlantic steamer approaches New York. The English cabin stewardess is unwittingly implicated in a smuggling attempt by a pair of American counterfeiters and narrowly escapes arrest. Her humiliating strip-search is rendered with a chilling immediacy that suggests the direction Catherine might have taken, had she continued writing fiction in America.

18 The *Overland Monthly* was founded in 1868 and flourished under the editorship of Bret Harte and Ina Coolbrith. It ceased publication in 1875 and resumed in 1883.

19 See Englekin, Bernhardine.

20 Guido Reni (1575–1642) was an Italian painter whose fresco *Phoebus and the Hours Preceded by Aurora* was considered his masterpiece.

21 Hero of John Bunyan's *Pilgrim's Progress* (1678).

22 Catherine's stepmother, Martha Lloyd Austen.

23 Dock warrants: Catherine apparently refers to documents authorizing the release of funds by John Heath, who administered the assets of her marriage to the incapacitated John Hubback.

24 A lighter version of the stagecoach, suitable for muddy roads and mountainous terrain.

25 A four-wheeled carriage with two seats and standing room on top.

26 See Calaveras Big Trees.

27 The Concord Coach, the iconic stagecoach widely used by Wells Fargo, was manufactured in Concord, New Hampshire.

28 A 'carriage with benches': a horse-drawn omnibus, often used for sightseeing.

29 A three-volume format was typical of Victorian novels, including Catherine's own.

30 The Ransom Fair was organized by San Francisco's French community to raise a contribution toward the indemnity demanded by Prussia at the end of the Franco-Prussian War (1870–1).

31 See St Mary of the Immaculate Conception Church.

32 See Carr, Ezra. In England the name 'Kerr' is commonly pronounced 'Carr.'

33 See University of California.

34 See Mills Seminary.

35 In the presidential election of 1872, the incumbent Republican, Ulysses S. Grant, was challenged by the nominee of the dissident Liberal Republicans: newspaper editor and former New York congressman, Horace Greeley. Grant won the popular vote on 5 November, and Greeley died three weeks later.

36 Pope Pius IX.

37 Henry Edward Manning was Roman Catholic Archbishop of Westminster at the time of Catherine's reference. He had left the Anglican Church in 1851 and would be named a cardinal in 1875.

38 See Holy Trinity Church.

39 Three publications of Harper & Brothers were popular in Catherine's time. Politics was the focus of *Harper's Weekly*, which supported Grant. *Harper's New Monthly Magazine* published extracts from current literature, while *Harper's Bazar* (later *Bazaar*) was devoted to fashion and offered patterns in a weekly supplement.

40 The ironclad *CSS Alabama*, built in Birkenhead for the Confederate States Navy, menaced Federal shipping during the American Civil War. Damages of $15,000,000 were awarded to the United States.

41 See Havens, Frank.

42 Louis Figuier was a French scientist who wrote widely on occult subjects. *The Tomorrow of Death: The Future Life According to Science* appeared in English in 1872.

43 Emanuel Swedenborg (1688–1772) was a Swedish scientist and theologian. Of his many books, only one, *Divine Providence*, was available in English in Catherine's time.

44 Acacia trees.

45 George John Douglas Campbell, 8th Duke of Argyll (1823–1900), was a Scottish peer and Liberal statesman, well versed in science. Although on respectful terms with Charles Darwin, he opposed his theory of evolution. In *The Reign of Law* (1866) and other writings he argued in favor of a divine creator.

46 Catherine's fifth novel: *Malvern, or The Three Marriages*.

47 John Stuart Mill was an English philosopher and economist. *The Subjection of Women*, published in 1865, presented a strong case for women's suffrage.

48 Aria for soprano in Vincenzo Bellini's opera *Norma* (1831).

49 The quadrille, danced by a 'set' of four of more couples, was imported from France to England in the early years of the nineteenth century and was therefore known to Catherine from childhood. Its variant, the Lancers, appeared in England in 1850. The Sir Roger de Coverly, an English country dance from the seventeenth century, became fashionable in London in the 1840s. All six ladies present at Mrs Blair's party would have been required to complete a set, with a line of facing gentlemen. An American version of the dance is called the Virginia Reel.

50 Tubular glass beads used to ornament women's clothing.

51 Fanny Squeers, a character in Charles Dickens's 1839 novel *The Life and Adventures of Nicholas Nickleby*, is the ill-favored daughter of the cruel schoolmaster Wackford Squeers. She is

described as 'almost handsome' in a scene where Nickleby, with whom she is infatuated, rebuffs her.

52   The satirical weekly *Punch*, founded in 1841, combined humor with political commentary. By the 1850s its anti-establishment character had given way to a more conservative viewpoint, notable for its anti-Irish bias.

53   Hampshire.

54   Ulysses S. Grant.

55   Probably *fanchon* (kerchief).

56   See Austen, Janet Rose.

57   See Mount Diablo.

58   See Austen, Francis George Heathcote.

59   Another incorrect version of *fanchon*.

60   See Sierra Nevada.

61   See Austen, Ernest Leigh.

62   William Henry Lytton Earle Bulwer, Baron Dalling and Bulwer (1801–72) was a diplomat whose postings included three years as ambassador in Washington. He died before completing his *Life of Palmerston*, of which Volumes I and II appeared in 1870.

63   Henry John Temple, Third Viscount Palmerston, left the Tory Party in 1830. He served twice as prime minister: 1855–8 and 1859–65. At the time of his visit, Catherine was seventeen years old.

64   Of the members of the grebe family of aquatic birds, the western grebe was a likely source of plumage for Catherine's cape. Fashion-driven demand for 'grebe fur' (breast plumage) and head plumes had by 1860 brought the great-crested grebe to the brink of extinction in England.

65   Alice Maud Mary (1843–78), grand duchess of Hesse-Darmstadt, was the third child of Queen Victoria and Prince Albert. At the time of Catherine's writing, Princess Alice was in mourning for her youngest son.

66 Catherine's brother-in-law, Joseph Hubback, was Mayor of Liverpool from 1869 to 1870. This trip was his third to North America.

67 Probably a reference to Tory Prime Minister Benjamin Disraeli's role in securing British control of the Suez Canal.

68 Joseph Alexander Hübner (1811–92) was an Austrian diplomat whose account of an eight-month journey (*Promenade autour du Monde* by M. le Baron de Hübner) was published in English in 1871 as *A Ramble round the World*.

69 This chain-stitch sewing machine, patented in 1857 by James Gibbs and improved by J. Willcox, was widely popular in America. The lock-stitch machine of the Canadian Wanzer Company, founded in 1858, won prizes at European expositions.

70 Bodice: the fitted part of a dress that extends from the waist to the shoulder.

71 Perhaps a reference to Tom Bailey, narrator of *The Story of a Bad Boy*. The 1869 novel by Thomas Bailey Aldrich was cited by Samuel Clemens (Mark Twain) as the inspiration for his own book *The Adventures of Tom Sawyer*, published in June 1876.

72 St John's Episcopal Church supported small congregations, known as missions, in sparsely populated areas of Oakland such as Temescal and Oakland Point.

73 The San Francisco Laundry Ordinance of 1873 imposed a $2 fee on laundries with animal-drawn carts. For laundries without carts (primarily those of Chinese ownership), the fee was increased to $15.

74 Centennial celebration of the signing of the Declaration of Independence from Great Britain on 4 July 1776.

75 Ivory tiles or cards upon which letters are inscribed. These are arranged to form words or phrases: a popular pastime in the Austen family and probably introduced to Catherine and

her sisters by their aunt Cassandra. A memorable account appears in Jane Austen's novel *Emma*.

76 Probably a reference to a needlework memorial to Mary's nephew, to which she, her elder sister Caroline, and others contributed.

77 Catherine refers to the south of England, where her father cultivated grapes at Portsdown Lodge.

78 *The Book of Days*, published in 1869 by Robert Chambers, is a wide-ranging compendium of information, organized day by day. 'Jane Austen, novelist' appears twice, on the anniversaries of her birth and death.

79 Eucalyptus trees.

80 In the 7 November election, Democrat Samuel Tilden won the popular vote by a narrow majority over Republican Rutherford B. Hayes, but electoral votes in four states were disputed. By the date of Catherine's letter, committees to resolve the issue had been formed in the Senate and House of Representatives. Two months of contentious negotiations ended on 2 March 1877, when Hayes was declared President.

Members of the Austen Family Mentioned in the Letters

1 Deirdre Le Faye, '*Sanditon*: Jane Austen's Manuscript and Her Niece's Continuation,' *Review of English Studies*, New Series, XXXVIII, 149 (February 1987), pp. 56–60.

BIBLIOGRAPHY

Austen, Caroline, *Reminiscences of Caroline Austen*, introduction by Deirdre Le Faye (Guildford: The Jane Austen Society, 1986).

Austen, Jane, *Jane Austen's Letters*, new edition, ed. Deirdre Le Faye (Oxford: Oxford University Press, 1995).

Austen-Leigh family collection, 23M93, Hampshire Record Office, Winchester.

Austen-Leigh, James Edward, *A Memoir of Jane Austen*, second edition (London: Richard Bentley and Son, 1871).

Austen-Leigh, Richard Arthur, *Pedigree of Austen* (privately printed, 1940). Reprinted, London: Routledge/Thoemmes Press, 1995, with an introduction by David Gilson.

Bagwell, Beth, *Oakland: The Story of a City* (Novato: Presidio Press, 1982).

Beidleman, Richard G., *California's Frontier Naturalists* (Berkeley: University of California Press, 2006).

Bohakel, Charles A., *A Pictorial Guidebook to Mount Diablo* (privately printed, 1975).

Chapman, R. W., *Jane Austen: Facts and Problems*, the Clark Lectures, Trinity College, Cambridge, 1948 (Oxford: The Clarendon Press, 1950).

Chapman, R. W. (ed.), *The Watsons: A Fragment* (Oxford: The Clarendon Press, 1927). Reprinted, London: The Athlone Press, 1985.

Corder, Joan, 'Akin to Jane' (unpublished manuscript, Jane Austen's House Museum, Chawton).

Davis, Michael, 'Jane Austen and Cricket,' *The Jane Austen Society Report for 2000*, pp. 24–8.

Decker, Peter R., *Fortunes and Failures: White-Collar Mobility in Nineteenth-Century San Francisco* (Cambridge, MA: Harvard University Press, 1978).

Dutton, Joan Parry, *They Left their Mark: Famous Passages through the Wine Country*, second edition (Calistoga: Sharpsteen Museum Association, 1998).

Gibson, Ross Eric, 'A First in Hot Bathing – How a War and a Divorce Figured in the Birth of the Boardwalk in 1868,' *San Jose Mercury News*, 13 July 1993, 1B. Published online, n.d., <http://www.santacruzpl.org/history/articles/343/>, accessed 8 March 2010.

Gisel, Bonnie Johanna, *Kindred and Related Spirits: The Letters of John Muir and Jeanne C. Carr* (Salt Lake City: University of Utah Press, 2001).

Grierson, Janet, *Dr. Wilson and his Malvern Hydro: Park View in the Water Cure Era* (Malvern: Cora Weaver, 1998).

Hall-Jones, Roger, *The Story of Park View Malvern* (Malvern: First Paige, 1998).

Hodgson, Susan F., *A Geysers Album: Five Eras of Geothermal History* (Sacramento: California Department of Conservation, Division of Oil, Gas, and Geothermal Resources, 1997).

Hopkinson, David, 'A Niece of Jane Austen,' *Notes and Queries*, 229 (December 1984), pp. 470–1.

—— 'The Watsons,' in *The Jane Austen Companion*, ed. J. David Grey, (London: The Athlone Press, 1986).

—— *The Watsons: A Novel by Jane Austen and Another* (London: Peter Davies Limited, 1977).

Hopkinson, Diana, 'Peepshow on Victorian Life: Catherine Hubback's Sketchbooks,' *Country Life*, 30 March 1978.

Hopkinson, Diana and David Hopkinson, 'Niece of Miss Austen' (unpublished typescript of 271 pages, Hopkinson deposit, Jane Austen's House Museum, Chawton).

Hubback, Catherine, *Agnes Milbourne* (London: Charles J. Skeet, 1856).

—— *Life and Its Lessons* (London: William Shoberl, 1851).

—— *Malvern, or The Three Marriages* (London: Charles J. Skeet, 1855).

—— *May and December* (London: Charles J. Skeet, 1854).

—— *The Mistakes of a Life* (London: Thomas Cautley Newby, 1863).

—— *The Old Vicarage* (London: Charles J. Skeet, 1856).

—— *The Rival Suitors* (London: Charles J. Skeet, 1857).

—— *The Stage and the Company* (London: Charles J. Skeet, 1858).

—— 'The Stewardess' Story,' *Overland Monthly*, October 1871, pp. 337–43.

—— *The Wife's Sister, or The Forbidden Marriage* (London: William Shoberl, 1851).

—— *The Younger Sister* (London: Thomas Cautley Newby, 1850).

Hubback, John, *A Treatise on the Evidence of Succession to Real and Personal Property and Peerages* (London: William Benning & Co., 1844).

Hubback, John H., *Cross Currents in a Long Life* (Bedford: Rogers G. Porter Limited, The Castle Press, 1935).

—— 'Eddies from Cross Currents of a Long Life' (unpublished typescript of 79 pages supplied to me by Diana and David Hopkinson in December 2000), 1938.

Hubback, John H. and Edith C. Hubback, *Jane Austen's Sailor Brothers* (London: John Lane, 1906).

Hubback, John H. and G. J. S. Broomhall, *Corn Trade Memories: Recent and Remote* (Liverpool: Northern Publishing Co., 1930).

Kelly, E. S., *Condensed Sketch of the Early History of California, San Francisco, and Oakland* (Oakland: Pacific Press, 1879).

Kemble, John Haskell, *San Francisco Bay: A Pictorial Maritime History* (Cambridge, MD: Cornell Maritime Press, 1947). Reprinted, New York: Bonanza Books, 1978.

Kirkham, Ralph W., *The Mexican War Journal and Letters of Ralph Kirkham*, ed. Robert Ryal Miller (College Station: Texas A & M University Press, 1991).

LaBounty, S. W., 'The Great Race,' posted 20 December 2000, <http://www.outsidelands.org/sw6.php>, accessed 8 March 2010.

Lamott, Kenneth, *Who Killed Mr. Crittenden?* (New York: David McKay Company, Inc., 1963).

Lane, Maggie, *Jane Austen's Family through Five Generations* (London: Robert Hale Limited, 1984).

Le Faye, Deirdre (ed.), *Jane Austen's Letters* (Oxford: Oxford University Press, 1995).

Le Faye, Deirdre, '*Sanditon*: Jane Austen's Manuscript and Her Niece's Continuation,' *Review of English Studies*, New Series, XXXVIII, 149 (February 1987), pp. 56–60.

Le Faye, Deirdre and W. and R. A. Austen-Leigh, *Jane Austen: A Family Record* (London: British Library, 1989).

Lewis, Oscar (ed.), *This Was San Francisco* (New York: David McKay Company, Inc., 1962).

Mitchell, Sally, *Daily Life in Victorian England* (Westport, CT: Greenwood Press, 1996).

Nicolson, Nigel, *The World of Jane Austen* (London: George Weidenfeld & Nicolson Ltd, 1991). Reprinted in paperback, London: Phoenix Illustrated, 1997.

Nordhoff, Charles, *California: for Health, Pleasure, and Residence: A Book for Travellers and Settlers* (New York: Harper & Brothers, 1873). Reprinted in paperback as *California for Travellers and Settlers*, Berkeley: Ten Speed Press, 1974.

Norris, Frank, *The Octopus*, edited with an introduction by Kenneth S. Lynn (Boston: Houghton Mifflin, 1958).

Perry, Claire, *Pacific Arcadia: Images of California 1600–1915* (New York: Oxford University Press, 1999).

Rapson, Richard L. (ed.), *Britons View America:Travel Commentary, 1860–1935* (Seattle: University of Washington Press, 1971).

Simons, John, *A History of Cricket in Hampshire, 1760–1914*, Hampshire Papers, 4 (Winchester: Hampshire County Council, 1993).

Stadtman, Verne A. (ed.), *The University of California 1868–1968* (New York: McGraw-Hill Book Company, 1970).

Starr, Kevin, *Americans and the California Dream, 1850–1915* (New York: Oxford University Press, 1973).

Saxon, Isabelle [Mrs Redding Sutherland], *Five Years within the Golden Gate* (London: Chapman and Hall, 1868).

Stillwell, B. F., *Directory of the Township and City of Oakland, together with the Townships of Brooklyn and Alameda for the Year 1869* (Oakland: *Oakland News* office, 1869). Updated editions published annually thereafter.

Sutherland, John, *The Stanford Companion to Victorian Fiction* (Stanford: Stanford University Press, 1989).

—— *Victorian Fiction: Writers, Publishers, Readers* (New York: St Martin's Press, 1995).

Thompson, Thomas H. and Albert A. West, *Historical Atlas of Alameda County, California* (Oakland: Thompson and West, 1878). Reprinted, Fresno: Valley Publishers, 1976.

Tomalin, Claire, *Jane Austen: A Life* (New York: Viking, 1997). Published in paperback, London: Penguin Books Ltd, 1998.

Trollope, Frances, *Domestic Manners of the Americans* (London: Whittaker, Treacher & Co., 1832).

Tucker, George Holbert, *A Goodly Heritage: A History of Jane Austen's Family* (Manchester: Carcanet New Press, 1983).

Wardle, Patricia, *Victorian Lace* (London: Jenkins, 1968). Revised second edition, Carlton, Bedford: Ruth Bean, 1982.

Wheeler, Kate Kirkham, unpublished letters to Jane Voiles, Oakland History Room, Oakland Public Library, 1942.

INDEX